Breathless

AN AMERICAN GIRL IN PARIS

NANCY K. MILLER

SEAL PRESS

BREATHLESS
An American Girl in Paris

Published by
Seal Press
A Member of the Perseus Books Group
1700 Fourth Street
Berkeley, California
www.sealpress.com

Library of Congress Cataloging-in-Publication Data

Miller, Nancy K., 1941-
   Breathless : an American girl in Paris / by Nancy K. Miller.
      pages cm
   ISBN 978-1-58005-488-1 (paperback)
1. Miller, Nancy K., 1941- 2. Americans—France—Paris—Biography. 3.
Young women—France—Paris—Biography. 4. Coming of age—Case studies. 5.
Autonomy—Case studies. 6. Miller, Nancy K., 1941—Relations with men. 7. Paris
(France)—Biography. 8. Paris (France)—Social life and customs—20th century. 9.
Young women—New York (State)—New York—Biography. I. Title.
   DC705.M55A3 2013
   944'.3610836092—dc23
   [B]
                                    2013016144

9 8 7 6 5 4 3 2 1

Cover design by Kimberly Glyder
Interior design by Domini Dragoone
Eiffel Tower art © sarella/123rf, fleur de lys art © Victor Kunz/123rf
Printed in the United States of America
Distributed by Publishers Group West

For Kamy Wicoff

You NEVER GET OVER YOUR first great love, Colette says in one of her novels, alluding to the wounds inflicted by the first of her three husbands. Tucked away in a secret compartment, that kind of hurt lives on—a permanent resident with a lifetime visa. How could the circuits of hope have collapsed so quickly, you wonder, stunned by the evidence of your misery? When did the paths leading to the happy ending veer off into a labyrinth of despair? The answers never match the questions. You just know that you won't ever be the same. Eventually, that's the good news. I never got over Paris. In the beginning, the pain of separation was acute, but in the end I've found a way to make a story out of it. After a while, of course, you believe the story you tell about your life. True story, the author says on the book jacket. In other words, before it was a story, it was also real.

I went to Paris because I was enamored of the sexy nouvelle vague movies, which, like the eighteenth-century novels I had read in college, offered entry into scenarios of freedom barred to me as long as I lived at home. I wanted to smoke in a Left Bank café. I wanted to be sophisticated and daring, nothing like my nice-Jewish-girl self and her nice Jewish parents from whom I longed to escape. But the strangest thing—and I was quite blind to the paradox then—was that in going to Paris I wound up even more hopelessly entangled with my parents, who had made Paris a world of their own well before I arrived on the scene. In the end, I had to leave Paris, if I wanted to be free.

I've been haunted by the girl in this book for most of my life. Now that those years of the 1960s when Paris loomed so large on my fantasy screen are securely locked away in the past, and reordered by memory, I've finally come to see her as someone I can forgive for trying so hard to become someone she was never meant to be: an eighteenth-century marquise, or more modernly, a girl whose wardrobe included a striped Dior shirtwaist dress.

My First French Lover

I DIDN'T SET OUT TO sleep with Philippe. For one thing, he was my parents' friend; for another, he was married.

On one of their many trips to Paris before I lived there, my parents met Philippe Roussel, an ophthalmologist, at Aux Charpentiers, a neighborhood restaurant near Saint-Germain des Près, where long, family-style tables bring you into closer contact with other diners than you might wish. In his travel diary, which I discovered after his death, my father reported that the French friends who had recommended the restaurant had said that "while not modern or elegant it was a place where intellectuals came to eat."

My parents were all for intellectuals, as long as I didn't marry one. And while traveling in France, which they had been doing since the mid-1950s, they prided themselves on eating at restaurants not listed in the *Michelin Guide*. Sitting across the narrow table, the doctor noticed my father putting drops into his bloodshot eyes. He struck up a conversation with my parents, offering his professional services. After dinner they all went back to his office around the corner on the rue Jacob, where the eye doctor treated my father by injection. As if that were not enough ("This could only happen to me," my father noted in a rare burst of personal reporting), Philippe then invited my parents into his living quarters adjacent to the office for drinks and music. Philippe, it turned out, was not only a great eye doctor but a brilliant pianist. He played from memory for an hour. The music so moved my father that he crushed the wine glass he was holding in his hand. The following year, when they became better acquainted, Philippe played tennis with my mother, who was not accustomed to losing, and beat her 6–2, 6–2, 6–4, "a fine game," according to the diary entry, despite the score.

I never knew what I liked most about the story, which my father had told more than once: my father having his eye injected by a total stranger, or my father so stirred by Schubert that he broke a glass listening to the music.

When I arrived in Paris in the early fall of 1961 to study at the Sorbonne, I made an appointment to see Philippe about my contact lens prescription. A few weeks later he invited me to a party at his apartment. The following day, when I got back from my job teaching English at a lycée for girls, I found his card with a message scrawled in brown ink: "*N. Vous avez fait des ravages.*" The ravaged victim of my charms turned out to be a Japanese painter who had been passing through Paris. He wanted to practice his English over dinner, but I wasn't in the mood for more lessons. Within the week, Philippe invited me out to dinner himself. We drove to Montparnasse in his red Volkswagen convertible with the top up and his hand under my skirt.

I wasn't completely surprised to find Philippe's hand creeping nimbly under my garter belt. I had already been initiated into this practice by Monsieur Delattre, the phonetics professor, during the summers I spent at Middlebury College's French School, where all the students signed a Language Pledge—*un engagement d'honneur*—not to speak a word of English for six weeks, under threat of expulsion. We were willing prisoners of the Pledge, endlessly correcting each other, alert to the slightest infraction, even while kissing. "Perfecting" our French was the fantasy that inspired compliance.

Monsieur Delattre would pick me up at my boarding house and we would go for long drives late at night down deserted country roads. I learned French slang words for penis—*queue* and *verge,* surprised that they were feminine nouns, while *con,* "cunt," was masculine, and also meant a guy who was a jerk—with no clue that nice girls were not supposed to know those expressions, certainly not use them. I cared only about my accent and getting the gender right. I justified the fingers by the phonetics. As it turned out, the French professor's hand-in-the-crotch-while-driving routine on Vermont country roads proved to be excellent preparation for my first year in Paris. I almost didn't mind being another stop on a stick shift. There was something seductive and guiltless about being a good pupil.

After an extra rare steak au poivre washed down with a bottle of Saint-Julien at the Coupole, we drove back to Philippe's apartment. He poured champagne for both of us and played a late Schubert sonata, cigarette drooping French-style from his mouth, the ash dropping slowly over the piano keys. I didn't break a glass, but I was impressed. Philippe had hesitated between the conservatory and medical school, he told me. A little after eleven o'clock, he stopped playing and suggested—very quietly—that I spend the night. I can't say that I found Philippe physically attractive—tall, thin, with a long beaky nose and thin lips—but he somehow forced you to like his ugliness.

"It's late, you know. If you leave now, you'll disturb the concierge."

"But you're married." The concierge was the least of my concerns.

"Anne has gone to the mountains with our son. She won't be back for two weeks."

"But wouldn't she mind?"

"That's my problem, not yours. If it doesn't bother me, why should it bother you?"

I knew from the French movies I had seen that the more you talk about it, the further you commit yourself to doing the very thing you say you neither wish nor intend to do.

"I'll be careful," Philippe continued, softly, taking advantage of my silence. "So what can happen?"

"But," I lamely started and stopped. Philippe had a subtle voice that ranged between irony and caress that was hard to resist.

"Darling, you're not a child. Tell me, what could happen?"

"Nothing."

"So if nothing can happen and no one finds out, no one will get hurt, right?"

"Right," I said, reluctantly, though I knew it couldn't be that simple.

"So why not?"

I could never find a strong rejoinder to "Why not?"

Philippe drew me a bath in the most beautiful bathroom I had ever seen. The walls were painted a dark eggplant lacquer. They gleamed. Philippe sat on the edge of the tub in his white terry cloth robe, smoking and pouring a capful of Obao bath oil beads that turned the water turquoise blue. After watching me for a while without speaking, he brought me a robe that matched his (the kind I had only seen in the expensive hotels my parents liked to stay at), and holding hands, we walked slowly down the carpeted corridor in silence to the bedroom.

We lay on the bed, kissed lightly, and shared a last cigarette. Still not speaking, Philippe climbed on top of me and, within a matter of minutes of intense activity, rolled off neatly with a small groan. He took a cigarette out of his pack, tapped it lightly, and lit up.

"Et moi?" I asked, startled by the smoke signals that suggested closure. Philippe dragged on his cigarette, and offered me a puff. It wasn't about smoking, but I couldn't find the words. I took a cigarette from my own pack instead, and lay silent in the darkness. This was not what happened in any of the foreign movies I had seen.

"Débrouillez-vous," he said, after a while, propping himself up on one elbow. He pointed languidly to my other hand, which seemed to mean that if I wanted more, the rest was up to me.

"Do it myself? Is that something French?" I finally asked, torn between humiliation and curiosity.

"Oh," Philippe said fondly in English, "American girl," as though the answer should be obvious.

"Only until I know whether it's going to be a *passade*," he added, "or something serious."

A passing fancy. I wondered how he decided. As I fell asleep, I forced myself not to think about Philippe's wife.

The next morning the Swedish au pair brought us breakfast in bed: café au lait and warm croissants with butter and jam. I was stunned as much by the elegance of the breakfast (beautifully laid out on the tray, with simple white bowls and pitchers of coffee and hot milk) as by their complicity. (When did he tell her what to do, and wouldn't she mention his overnight guest to his wife?) But I didn't ask these questions (Did he sleep with her too?) and instead acted as though I understood the rules of the game, as though I did this sort of thing all the time. After breakfast, Philippe placed the tray outside the bedroom door, as if we had spent the night in a hotel, and started up again. Afterward, he took my face between his lovely long hands and wiped away the crumbs on my lips.

"You're a sweet girl. You turn me on," Philippe declared, kissing me.

Then he walked down the hallway that led to his day as a doctor in the other part of the apartment. "Let yourself out," he said, his hand on the doorknob. "You'll come to dinner when Anne gets back. I'm sure she'll want to meet you. You'll like her. She adores your parents," he added, as if to reassure me.

I walked back slowly through the elegant streets of Saint-Germain. It was briefly sunny that morning and I sat for a while on a rented chair in the Luxembourg Gardens, watching the children sail their tiny boats in the pond despite the cold. Was this the beginning of a story or a one-night stand? A passionate affair or a *passade*? When would I know? This was, I had begun to see, the problem with "experimenting," my parents' code word for what they took to be my vast sexual experience. By definition, there was no way to know beforehand how an experiment would turn out. If Philippe was typical of French lovers, I was headed for disappointment. He seemed to have performed better on the tennis court with my mother.

"I went to a party at Anne and Philippe's house last night," I reported the next day in my weekly letter. "They served blanc de blanc and foie gras." (I actually wrote "*foie de gras.*" Those were early days.) "I met a charming Japanese painter, who wants me to teach him English."

If I had gone to Paris to escape from my parents, it had not taken me long to return home in my mind, even through my lies.

Waiting for Godard

I HAD LEFT NEW YORK for Paris still under the spell of *Breathless*. Godard's new wave movie, which my boyfriend David had taken me to see on my twentieth birthday, had made everything French infinitely desirable, as if I needed any persuading. Jean Seberg's character, Patricia, seemed self-possessed, independent, and unafraid, three things I desperately wanted to be. Patricia looked as if she had happily traded innocence for experience some time ago. She had cropped hair, a tight tee-shirt over capri pants, and lovers she wasn't even sure she loved.

Playing a girl from New York on her own in Paris, Jean Seberg was the quintessential gamine, and then there was her bad boyfriend. Within minutes of seeing them on the screen, Jean-Paul Belmondo and Jean Seberg eclipsed the Jean-Paul Sartre and Simone de Beauvoir couple ideal I had nourished in college: the template for the intellectual life that included sex while excluding marriage. Belmondo's character

Michel was the opposite of intellectual, of course, but I was attracted to the danger he brought to their relations.

Patricia was enrolled in courses at the Sorbonne as I would be (the price of parental financial support), but it was obvious from the start that going to school didn't take up much of her time. She was too busy trying to be a journalist. I loved the idea of the girl in the black-and-white-striped (Dior) shirtwaist dress jumping out of a stolen car and rushing off to a press conference for a celebrity novelist at Orly. During the interview with the great man, who sported dark glasses and a hat, Seberg veiled her ambition behind her own sunglasses, chewing nervously on her pencil, before daring to ask the writer whether he thought women had a role to play in the modern world. But when asked what she was doing in Paris, Patricia replied that she was writing a novel. I studied my expression in the bathroom mirror as she did and, holding my breath, rehearsed her answer. I discovered that if the words went by fast enough, I almost believed them. If I didn't write a novel, at least I would live one.

In Paris, I would leave my boring Barnard-girl self behind in Manhattan along with my parents. France was my hedge against the Marjorie Morningstar destiny that haunted American girls in the 1950s: marriage to a successful man and then the suburbs with children. In exchange for financing the year in Paris, my parents had exacted their particular pound of flesh: an account of my comings and goings in the form of a weekly letter. Letter writing seemed a small enough price to pay for the thrill of being in Europe. The harder part was the promise, in their words, not to hide anything from them. I promised, figuring that there was no way for them to ferret out any hidden items now that I wasn't living under their roof. Besides, I was a literary girl. I had read epistolary novels. I could easily turn out the kinds of letters that would dazzle with detail while omitting the truth. I had written enough of them from summer camp where the weekly letter home was obligatory, considering how much it had cost the parents to pack the kids off to the Adirondacks for eight weeks.

When I emptied my parents' apartment after their deaths, I found my letters from Paris tied in a little bundle sitting in a drawer next to the letters from my years at Camp Severance. Seeing the two packets of epistolary history, arranged in chronological order, adjacent to each other in my mother's dresser, made me think that for her the two correspondences were comparable objects—and perhaps they were, even if in my mind the experiences, each lasting six years, belonged to entirely different eras, not to say selves. Both sets of letters home seemed designed to produce a certain effect—to make my parents think their daughter was having a good time, and that beyond the long string of items necessary to further survival that only they could supply, I didn't need them or miss them. I was away: a happy camper. Happy at age nine, or twenty.

When I reread the Paris letters, I quickly saw the fatal flaw in my decision to hide what my parents wanted to know. What exactly was I concealing from scrutiny? I sensed, hidden in the landscape of elaborate detail, the traces of the very feelings I passionately wanted to recover in order to reconstruct my past. Naturally, as a writer I loved the documentation: the pale blue sweater I bought at the Galeries Lafayette ("I feel so authentic when I wear it!"); the play by Brecht, the Resnais movie I saw (so avant-garde); the new, darker, "Russian" color of my hair. But if I wanted to know what the hyperbole (wonderful, marvelous, fantastic!!!) and the exclamation marks—my favorite form of punctuation—were masking, I would have to reimagine my life as the American girl I was, except in my own eyes.

I HAD BEEN DESPERATE TO leave home for college and live on campus as most of my friends were planning to do. But with their uniquely Jewish brand of casuistry, their uncanny ability to make me disbelieve my own reality, my parents conned me into accepting their bargain: rather than buy into the expensive clichés of dormitory life—how American!—with the money they would be saving for me, I could study in France after graduation. Wasn't Europe the dream? (Yes.) Didn't that make more sense? (Not really.)

I lived at home and attended Barnard.

How did they convince me that I didn't want what I wanted? The pattern had set in when I was young, and years of being talked out of my desires (patent leather Mary Janes were vulgar; so was tap dancing) had produced the desired effect. Together my parents had planted the seed of self-doubt in me so deeply, that no sooner did they question my wishes than I self-sabotaged. Was going away to school a waste of money? Was I too young? I no longer knew. I was suffering from a kind of Jewish Stockholm syndrome. I had to get away but somehow could not leave my captors, my parents to whom I was overly attached.

Paris was the consolation prize for four years of bitter daily skirmishes over the limits to my freedom.

The fact that only girls lived in Le Foyer International des Ètudi-antes made the arrangement acceptable to my parents, who seemed to hope I might still be a virgin, even though they talked as if I were already beyond the pale. Inspired in part by foreign movies and in part by *Les Liaisons Dangereuses,* the eighteenth-century libertine novel that the more literary boys at Columbia considered a handbook for seduction, I scorned the demi-vierges of our acquaintance, who at Barnard were majoring in virginity, as the phrase went. I set out to lose mine with David in my sophomore year, when I read the novel and declared my major in French. Still, there was a lot to learn. What counted after graduating from virginity was going further. I couldn't have said why—or how.

That was part of the plan for Paris. Finding out.

When I crossed the iron-gated threshold of the Le Foyer, carrying my pale blue matching suitcases, I quickly realized that I could redeem the time of my captivity by becoming someone I could not have become, doing what I could never have done—then.

Roommates

I WAS ASSIGNED A ROOMMATE, Monique Nataf, who came from a small seaport city in Tunisia.

"It's true that Mademoiselle Nataf is a foreigner," Madame la Directrice admitted reluctantly when I told her I would have preferred a French girl, "but she speaks French perfectly. In North Africa they do, you know," she added in a low voice.

Monique arrived a few days after I had settled into the room. Her first gesture was to cover her side of the room with reproductions of Renaissance paintings, portraits of women, mainly madonnas, looking inward and melancholy.

"Bellini?" I asked.

"I love Bellini, and you?"

"And me?"

"Who is your favorite painter?"

"Chagall," I said, anxious about the madonnas, and wishing I had said Matisse.

"I'm Jewish, too," she said, reading the question behind my answer. I blushed, but it was the first thing my parents had asked about Monique.

Monique had been born in France and lived in the Pyrenees during the Occupation. Her mother was Polish and grew up in Berlin; her father was from North Africa. Because she was born in France, Monique had a French passport, but in the eyes of the French French, we were both foreigners.

We were the same size and wore each other's clothing, playing at being sisters or even twins, despite the fact that Monique was as blonde as I was dark. It was the game of identification we liked. Monique's mother had been a *petite main*, an apprentice to a famous designer, when she was young. The dresses she made for Monique were a step above what my mother knocked out on the Singer sewing machine that provided the white noise to my childhood, and I coveted them.

One chilly afternoon, a street photographer snapped a picture of the two of us arm in arm. In the photograph, we are strolling down from the Foyer along the boulevard Saint-Michel, where girls were regularly pursued by relentless young men. "Vous êtes seules?" they would ask rhetorically, oblivious to our self-sufficiency. Alone! We're with each other! In the snapshot, Monique is wearing a double-breasted blazer, a straight skirt that falls just below the knee, sheer stockings that show off her slender legs, black pumps, leather gloves, and a perfectly tied scarf. She looks Parisian already and, like French girls, doesn't seem to feel the cold. Our arms are linked, but I'm dressed for another season, wearing the brown tweed wool dress with velvet piping that her mother made that fall (for both of us, we joked) and a beige, baggy corduroy coat I had still not realized was completely out of style in Paris.

The Foyer cast itself as the custodian of our virtue, the guardian of future wives and mothers. Madame Carnot, the cleaning woman, shared the Foyer's mission. One morning she knocked at the door at 7:30 while we were sitting on our beds, facing each other in our long flannel nightgowns. Monique opened the door, cigarette in hand.

Plunging her hands into the pockets of her smock, as she looked past Monique at the books and papers strewn across the floor, Madame Carnot threatened to report us to Madame la Directrice for bad conduct. She shook her head gravely to emphasize her point, and adjusted the little gray scarf she always wore to protect her hair.

I conjured up Jane Eyre's little friend Helen Burns wearing the sign for "slattern" in punishment for her untidy room.

"We are trying to form *femmes d'intérieur*," Madame Carnot added, unembarrassed by her identification with the *directrice*, who would have shuddered to share the pronoun. *Femmes d'intérieur* was one of those expressions that sounded better in French, more glamorous and seductive, but wasn't when you thought about it. We didn't want to be perfect housewives.

"Merci, madame." Monique shut the door, thanking the cleaning woman for the warning.

We didn't want to stay home and receive our husbands' guests. We wanted to read books during the day and go out every night. We wanted to have orgasms when we had sex. We didn't share that desire with Madame Carnot, of course. We barely admitted it to ourselves. But that was the only way in which either of us wanted to be women of the interior.

Nice Girls Don't Whistle

STUDENTS LIKE ME WHO WERE working toward a master's degree with the Middlebury program were required to attend a year of weekly lectures at the Sorbonne on *Les Liaisons Dangereuses*. The lectures on the novel were meant to provide the background for the *mémoire*, the research essay that was the cornerstone of the master's degree. We were expected to submit the outline (*le plan*) for the essay to a tutor early in the semester before starting to write. Unlike the American system in which you discovered what you thought while writing, feeling your way to an idea, in France you were expected to think first. I wasn't used to this.

I had been assigned a tutor who lived on the rue Lanneau, one of those dark streets behind the Pantheon, a short walk from the Foyer. We were encouraged to meet with our tutors once a week for two hours. Normally, those meetings took place during the day in the school offices at Montparnasse, but I had canceled my appointments for weeks because I couldn't find a topic, let alone write an outline. Finally, I was running out of time, and one day, as a special favor, my tutor, Monsieur Petitot, told me to come to his apartment after dinner to discuss the situation. We sat at the long oak table in his living room that served as a desk. Monsieur Petitot looked to be in his thirties, I thought, or maybe older, judging by his receding hairline and his gold-rimmed glasses. When he lit his pipe, I reached for my pack of Disque Bleu filtre and my notebook.

"So, mademoiselle," he began, still puffing on his pipe, "the outline?" I took a deep drag on my cigarette.

"That's the problem, monsieur. I don't have one."

The tutor frowned and played with his pipe. I noticed that his bottom teeth were turning brown at the top edges from the tobacco. I revised my estimate of his age. He must be pushing forty.

"Do you have a topic, at least?"

I said I was thinking about the women in the novel.

"Women aren't a topic."

I explained my idea that each of the three women characters is betrayed by the images others have of them and that they each have of themselves. I wasn't sure you could combine existentialism (that I more or less remembered from summer school) with libertinism (a big subject in the Laclos course), but the tutor nodded imperceptibly and told me to write it down.

As I fleshed out a proposal at the table, asking for approval at each stage before committing it to paper, Monsieur Petitot rose from his chair and walked around the room, pulling books off the shelves of his glass-enclosed bookcases and flipping through the pages, culling references for me as I scribbled. I could feel myself flying off on my own now, speeding, enthralled, dazzled by my insights. As I sat at the table bent over my notebook, I sensed the tutor's presence close to me. Monsieur Petitot came up quietly behind my chair, swiftly opened the first two buttons of my blouse, and cupped my left breast in his hand. I was still holding my pen. It was as if the tutor had taken me for Cécile, the ingénue in the novel, the girl who wore her feelings on her skin, the girl that all the characters manipulated with sickening ease. I was not as dumb as Cécile, but Monsieur Petitot was my teacher, and my whole plan for the future (not just *le plan*) depended on finishing my degree.

What was worse, saying no or saying yes? The hand circled slowly, cleverly inside my bra. I removed the hand.

"Oh, monsieur," I sighed, meaningfully, I hoped. "I have so many ennuis right now . . . I . . ." I trailed off, hoping the "now" would do the temporizing for me, afraid to anger the tutor with a no. He slowly removed his hand and squeezed my shoulder. I tilted my head toward the hand in a gesture of mute sympathy, as if I shared his regret. Monsieur Petitot showed me to the door, handing me my notebook and my copy of the novel. We shook hands politely and I promised to send him a draft in two weeks. When he closed the door behind me, I raced down the stairs and back to the Foyer.

Immediately inside the lobby of the Foyer was a desk with a switchboard and a sullen receptionist, who took messages and a dim view of the girls living there. I crossed the lobby floor to the staircase, whistling under my breath, jubilant with relief. I had a topic for my essay, and I had avoided sleeping with the tutor. The receptionist called me over before I could climb the stairs. "Mademoiselle." I approached the counter with a smile. "Mademoiselle, les jeunes filles ne sifflent pas." Nice girls don't whistle? Smoking in the street, I had already learned, was a *jeune fille* taboo. Not whistling was a new addition to my education.

Monique didn't think Monsieur Petitot would give me a bad grade, but I had read enough books to know that stories of girls who sleep with their tutors usually didn't end well.

Belmondo's Nose

Down one flight of stairs from the Foyer lobby was a restaurant open to all students, male and female—provided you had the *carte d'étudiant*, the precious student card that was our passport to the discounted life. Everyone complained about the food, of course, especially the gristly bits of stew that reminded us why the French were so devoted to sauces; we covered everything with mustard and washed it down with milk. But we were always hungry. Some afternoons, too ravenous to wait for dinner, Monique and I would head for a *salon de thé* not far from the Foyer to fill up on our favorite snack, a *vol-au-vent*. If we loved the way the heavy cream and mushrooms drenched the pastry shell, we loved as much being women on our own in a tearoom. *Parisiennes,* not just nice Jewish girls, as we had discovered in our first serious conversation at the Foyer. Women of the world, talking about men.

I had been invited to dinner a few times, as Philippe had said I would. I met Anne and several of their friends. Philippe would always kiss me good-bye at the door, pull me tight, say he'd be in touch, and ask to be remembered to my parents. But after a few weeks of silence, I realized that I must have turned out to be a *passade*.

"I think he prefers playing tennis with my mother to sleeping with me."

"Forget Philippe," Monique said, lighting a cigarette. Monique did not approve of affairs with married men, but she knew it was part of my libertine fantasy.

THREE LARGE BLACK MOTORCYCLES WERE often parked out in front of the Foyer at mealtimes. They belonged, we discovered, to three Americans who wore heavy black leather jackets and leather pants that hugged their legs. Everyone eyed the group as they ambled back to their bikes after lunch. After a couple of deep tokes on what looked more like dope than cigarettes, they would roar off down the boulevard Saint-Michel, weaving between the trucks and buses, never looking back at their little crowd of admirers still gathered on the pavement.

Early one afternoon, lured into the street by the unexpected warmth of Indian summer in late October, Monique and I stood outside the Foyer door, debating about taking a walk in the Luxembourg Gardens instead of going back upstairs to study in our room. One of the trio came over to us and asked me for a light—in English.

"Only if you take us for a ride," I said.

From certain angles, I thought, Leopold Gold (Leo, as he later told me to call him) resembled Jean-Paul Belmondo, especially the pouty fullness of his lips under a boxer's flattened, broken nose (Belmondo's, not Leo's, though it created the same impression). Leo's body was slender, and like Belmondo's radiated impatience. The hair, however, definitely was not French. The tight wave in the front said New York. I had spent years trying to eliminate the tribal kink from my own. It always came back, a rigid canopy over the forehead instead of a sexy, rebellious lock.

I climbed onto the hard leather seat behind Leo, Monique behind me. He headed down Saint-Michel, turning left on Saint-Germain, crossing the Seine to come out on Place de la Concorde, and then running up the Champs-Élysées to the Place de l'Étoile. Leo had taken us the tourist route to Paris's ultimate traffic jam, whose center was the Arc de Triomphe. Cars streamed into the circle at the center from the twelve streets that fed into the roundabout like the spokes of a wheel.

He turned to mouth "Dig this!" over the roar of traffic as he wove in and out, leaning into the turns. I clung to his waist; Monique squeezed mine. My contact lenses were burning from the dust of the hot afternoon. I knew my eyes were red. As we circled for the third time, a policeman hailed us. Leo pulled over and stopped the bike, his hands still on the handlebars, his heavy black boots lightly grazing the pavement. He looked up at the policeman with tiny pupils—the gaze of stoned, periwinkle innocence. "Deux, oui, trois, non," the officer began, glaring at the three of us. Faced with our smiling, blank faces, he kept repeating, "Deux, oui, trois, non!" gesticulating with his fingers to make the point, nodding and shaking his head for emphasis. It wasn't hard to catch his drift: according to the law two could ride on one bike, not three. We threw up our hands and chorused in English that we didn't understand what he was saying. Finally, the policeman waved us on in disgust, muttering about *les américains*. It pained me to pretend I didn't understand French, but better to be taken for ignorant American tourists who couldn't speak the language than have to produce our papers—all of us foreigners who could be thrown out anytime. The fear was real, even if Americans weren't among the most undesirable foreigners around.

"I think we can take the metro back," I said, when Leo started up the bike again. "It's only one change of trains." I would have been happy to change trains twice rather than mount his stallion, as he had referred to the bike with a straight face before taking off.

"As you like it, baby," Leo said, playing Belmondo to my Seberg.

Monique and I headed down the avenue, arm in arm, the picture, we hoped, of nonchalance, still trembling from the ride.

"I wonder if we'll see him again." Monique didn't answer. I knew she was thinking about Leo's friend, the blond biker.

"Do you want to?"

"I'm not sure." Something had happened on the ride, as though the danger had jump-started a relationship that suddenly felt sexual. Maybe it was just the enforced proximity, my breasts pressed against the back of a stranger.

It was November before we saw the bikes again. The weather had turned cold, and I remembered that Leo had talked about going to Italy before the days started shrinking into darkness. I was surprised that he hadn't already left town. When I went downstairs to the restaurant, I realized that I was looking forward to seeing him.

"Ça va?" Leo tapped me on the shoulder at the serving counter, as though we were picking up a lost thread. He pulled a tray off the top of the pile and put it down next to mine. I noted that Leo didn't seem to feel the need to explain his absence.

"So you live in the Foyer?" We had exchanged very few words on the bike. I nodded.

"And you?"

"Rue Monsieur le Prince," Leo said, smiling at the woman behind the counter, who piled up the meat and potatoes on his plate until they formed a small mountain.

"The Stella?" Monique's cousin also had a room there.

"I stayed at the Beat Hotel when I first came to Paris." I admired the almost seamless way he had worked the reference into the story. "But I never got to meet Kerouac."

I couldn't bring myself to admit I hadn't liked *On the Road*. It was such an American book, I thought, and all about guys in cars looking for their fathers. Still, Jack Kerouac was hip. That much I knew.

"Ginsberg and Corso were around when I was, though," he added, naming the Beat poets without their first names, as if I'd know. I nodded again.

"So what about dinner sometime?" Leo asked, as we separated at the end of the cafeteria line. "I'm going to Italy at the end of the month. I can't take the weather here. It's so fucking depressing." Leo was the first person I had met who placed "fucking" into a sentence as though it were a normal adjective. "How about Chez Ali?"

I had been to Chez Ali with Monique many times. One of her cousins knew the owner, who came from their town in Tunisia. The restaurant was a ten-minute walk from the Foyer.

WHILE LEO AND I WERE waiting to be served, I played with the curtains at the window next to our table, draping a linen panel over one side of my face.

"Veils and contact lenses don't go together," Leo said without smiling. "Especially not *green* contact lenses."

I flushed at being found out. I loved the "Oh, les beaux yeux," compliments I got on the boulevard whenever I wore them.

I bit into one of the dark green peppers sitting in a little dish of nibbles on the table. My tongue caught fire. I gulped down water, swallowing my embarrassment.

"Not water, bread," Leo said, passing me the basket.

Leo outlined his plan for the year, though "plan" was not quite the right word for his scenario. The deal, he said, was to be open to things as they happened and to be ready to move on. I liked that concept, though living it out might be another matter, I thought.

"What about school?" I asked, when he told me he had left Columbia with an unfinished master's essay on T.S. Eliot.

"First I have to see Greece and Turkey—then Israel."

"I thought you were going to Italy."

It was obvious for Leo that one country led to another. You just had to look at the map.

"And money?"

"I have a stash," Leo explained, from selling the hash he bought in Tangier. When he left the States, he had shipped his bike on a freighter to Tangier, where William Burroughs (another hero) was often in residence. "I can always deal a little on the side."

"Isn't that dangerous?" I asked, imagining my father's reaction to this information. "Don't expect us to visit you in jail."

Leo shrugged and dug into the steaming mountain of couscous in front of us.

I didn't want to treat him the way my parents treated me, demanding accounts of feelings and whereabouts, as though they were owed an explanation. With Leo, the roles were reversed. I pressed him—if only in my mind.

"What's dangerous is getting drafted," he said, with an edge of condescension. "Vietnam."

He walked me back to the Foyer, his arm thrown over my shoulder, as if something had been decided at dinner.

"You don't you miss anything about New York, not even Greenwich Village?"

"Baby, not Greenwich Village. The Village. Period. You're still just a nice little Barnard girl from Riverside Drive," he said with a mixture of tenderness and scorn. I knew the Village as well as he did. But Leo always assumed the role of the one who knew. And I went along with it.

When we arrived in front of the Foyer doors, Leo took my face in his hands and kissed me gently with his pillow lips. I wanted to ask him whether we would see each other before he left, but I knew that was not a cool chick thing.

Monique was reading *The Portuguese Letters* in bed. The letters were supposed to have been written by a Portuguese nun who was seduced and abandoned by a Frenchman, a soldier who had passed through town. Her letters to him from the convent went unanswered. They were heartbreaking, Monique and I agreed.

"Are you going to sleep with Leo?"

"It depends."

"On what?"

"On whether he asks me to meet him in Italy over Christmas."

Monique was going to Tunisia for the holidays. I didn't want to stay in Paris alone.

"But if he doesn't ask me, I won't. Sleep with him. I'll just stay here and work on the master's essay, which is what I should be doing anyway."

Would we or wouldn't we? How should we decide? That was always the question between us.

"I wish someone would leave me enough money so that I could live in Europe and never have to think of consequences," I continued, trying to explain my confusion.

Monique sighed, put the book down, and shut off the light.

"Money," she said, "that's so American."

Why did everything always come down to that? My being American? The point wasn't money; it was the problem of what my parents always called consequences, the running argument between us about everything I wanted to do, and would do, I believed, if it weren't for them. "Think of the consequences." I had come to Paris to get over the fear that their mantra might be right. Monique yearned for something absolute, irresistible, beyond practical considerations like geography or money. That's what made her European, she thought, and superior to me. It was too late to argue. I lay awake reviewing the kiss.

A FEW DAYS LATER I found a note from Leo at the front desk asking me to meet him at Le Bac, the café next door to the Foyer where I often had coffee with Monique in the morning. I immediately decided I would make the trip to Italy if he asked, even though I didn't know what it meant, or even what I wanted it to mean. Acting, not waiting, had become a matter of principle with me. Not that I wasn't waiting, of course. The trouble with existentialism, as far as I could tell, was that it worked better for men than for girls. I struggled to believe I could create myself by acting in the world alone. But even Simone de Beauvoir, looking back, said she had been waiting since she was fifteen for the "dream-companion" she found in Sartre. I had come to France, the land of my intellectual heroes, to live a passionate adventure of my own, but I seemed still to be taking baby steps, still waiting to be asked, while knowing this couldn't be the answer.

"SO WHAT DO YOU THINK?" Leo finally asked, stirring sugar into his *petit crème*.

"About what?" I asked back, wanting the question put into words. Leo hesitated as though he thought I was expecting him to propose marriage.

"You know, meeting me in Venice, baby." I had hoped for a little more language, but "baby" was going to have to do. "Why don't you ask Valerie to drive you? She just bought a car, didn't she?" Leo had met my classmate Valerie at a Thanksgiving party for Middlebury students.

"But you don't like her. You said she was uptight, or maybe even lesbian."

"But she likes you, baby, and if she gets you to Venice . . ." Leo didn't finish the sentence. I decided to take his pragmatism as an expression of his intense desire for me to make the trip.

How could I tell my parents I was going to Italy without putting Leo into the picture? They would try to discourage me if I said I was traveling alone (think of the consequences). I told them that a girl I knew from the Middlebury program was driving to Venice for the Christmas holidays and that she had asked me to join her. "Her father's a professor," I added, "a Renaissance art historian, specializing in Giotto." I wanted to round out the portrait in terms I knew my parents would find reassuring. My sister was majoring in art history. Giotto was already a household word.

No Sun in Venice

WE LEFT THE FIAT IN an open lot near the Piazzale di Roma and walked to the youth hostel where we planned to meet Leo for our first night in Venice. It was late and we decided to leave our suitcases in the car since we'd be moving to a hotel early the following day. By the next morning, when Valerie and I returned to pick up our luggage, the car had been picked clean. We stared at the empty car for a few minutes without speaking, stunned by our bad luck.

After two hours of declarations to the police, shrugged shoulders conveyed the official response to the plight of American girls leaving their belongings in a car with telltale TT license plates on Christmas Eve. "Peccato, signorine." That's a pity. Anyway, it was "la Festa," and everything was shut down for the holidays. Valerie glared at me as if I were entirely to blame, and maybe I was, given my true motive for luring her to Italy. I was less willing to take the blame in the required filial letter: "I'm worried that you'll think I'm irresponsible, etc. but is it really my fault?" I hated losing things, but I also hated knowing that by return mail my own feeling of loss would be drowned in the vast ocean of parental ire.

After our useless performance at the police station, we walked over to the Dorsoduro, where Leo had reserved two rooms at the Calcina, one for Valerie and me, and one for him. Valerie's father had suggested the Calcina, a *pensione* everyone who knew anything about art history preferred because John Ruskin had stayed there. The Calcina catered to American and English academics who couldn't begin to afford the legendary hotels like the Danieli, chosen by my parents, or more glamorously by George Sand and Alfred de Musset, who also traveled to Venice in winter. Still, the *pensione* faced the Guidecca canal and Leo had managed to get us rooms with a view.

When the stores reopened after the holidays, I walked into a small shop I had noticed near the Campo Santo Stefano, whose windows inspired daydreams of seduction. I fixated on what I took to be a slip of pale brown silk, trimmed in cream-colored lace, that would skim the top of the thighs. Too short for a skirt, too long to tuck into pants, the slip, if that's what it was, completed by matching bra and panties, seemed designed uniquely for dallying in a hotel room—filmed by Antonioni. The bra was made of two tiny triangular pieces of silk strung along a thin strap; the low-slung bikini panties formed a slender V at the crotch.

I hesitated at the counter, shocked by the price of the ensemble and embarrassed in my own eyes by the waist-high white cotton underpants I was wearing, and whose outline I was sure the saleswoman had deciphered through the dressing room door.

"Take beautiful things, *signorina*, and you can never go wrong," the saleswoman intoned, as if uttering a famous Italian maxim. I had been brought up on the opposite principle, inculcated in me by my mother through years of shopping from bins of clothing in the bargain basements she haunted. I had had a long apprenticeship at the crowded stores on Union Square, plunging my hand into the bottom of the pile ("You never know what you're going to find") to pluck out a treasure minus its original label (if, of course, you knew what the missing label was). I quickly cashed several traveler's checks' worth of lire as I pictured wearing the slip that night with Leo, feeling guiltier about spending the money than about "going to a man's room," in my father's preferred euphemism.

Of course, in my shopping fantasy the hotel room was not a bathroomless *pensione* above a restaurant, even if Ruskin had stayed there in another century.

I knocked on the door of Leo's room, down the hallway from the one Valerie and I were sharing. I held my new purchase up for inspection.

Leo nodded approval, but just kept sucking on his hash pipe, his pupils already pinpoints of satisfaction.

The first time we had sex, Leo reminded me of Philippe, minus breakfast in bed and the bathtub with blue water. Affectionate, but almost distracted, as though it wasn't the first time but the thirtieth, or as though we had stopped counting before we began. Leo's investment in sex was hard to decipher.

"Sex isn't everything," Leo said when I wondered aloud about what had (and hadn't) happened. "Besides, you'll get better, eventually." Why was pleasure again my job to figure out? And what exactly was the job description? Even speaking English, I couldn't bring myself to ask.

VENICE IN EARLY JANUARY WAS icy and misty, not the sublime white luminosity I had imagined. But we were happy to be tourists, crossing bridges, coming on hidden squares. "Speaking tons of Italian," I reported to my parents, hoping to make them feel that my Barnard education had paid off, despite the stolen suitcases, "actually constructing vaguely intelligent sentences."

As the three of us wandered through Piazza San Marco, almost deserted for the season, the cool rhythms of the Modern Jazz Quartet playing *No Sun in Venice* vibrated in my head. The album, a birthday present from David, had a Turner painting of the Grand Canal on the cover.

"You know, of course, that Vicenza is more important architecturally than Venice," David had written in his last letter from New York. I didn't see how that could be true, but I was used to taking his opinions seriously. We had broken up in late spring just before I left for France, but no sooner had I said the words "It's over" than I found myself wishing I could take them back, even though, as we both agreed, it was "impossible." We wanted different things, but maybe I had exaggerated our differences, maybe difference was good. The glue of ambivalence bonded our lack of resolution, our inability to make the break stick. The year away was supposed to clarify our feelings.

I told David I might be traveling to Italy at Christmas. I knew he wouldn't be able to resist the chance to make me a list of what I should see, even though he had never been there himself. The two of us had always had an epistolary relationship, even when we lived in the same city, a few blocks apart. It wasn't necessarily meaningful that we were writing again.

"We should really drive to Vicenza on Sunday," I said at dinner. "Vicenza is more important architecturally than Venice," I added, omitting David's "you know about Palladio, of course," but neither Leo nor Valerie protested.

Our time in Venice was almost over. We were all getting tired of walking around in the cold; Valerie and Leo were tired of each other. Maybe the change of scene would improve relations before we parted. Valerie and I would return to Paris from Vicenza. Leo could hitch a ride back to Venice and head for Rome alone on his motorcycle.

The windshield was frozen and the rear window was fogged. Valerie complained that she couldn't see a thing. From the backseat of the car, Leo offered to take the wheel.

"You can't drive my car when you're stoned," Valerie said, without turning her head, her foot on the break.

"Don't brake, just downshift." Being stoned never prevented Leo from giving advice.

I had decided to sit in the back with Leo, even though I knew Valerie would resent finding herself in the role of chauffeur. My head was in Leo's lap; I was ignoring the weather and Valerie's complaints. Leo continued to carry on a conversation with Valerie about the road. Suddenly, there was a crashing sound and the car skidded on the black ice, back-ending into a ditch on the side of the road. Then quiet.

We were alive! The three of us gingerly climbed out of the car, which seemed remarkably intact, though the back wheels were hopelessly jammed into the ditch.

"You should have downshifted," Leo repeated, extracting another joint from deep inside his jacket pocket, inspecting it for damage.

Valerie fumed. No words, just steamy puffs of cold air fogging her gold-rimmed glasses like angry smoke signals. I wanted to apologize, but I couldn't figure out what to say. We stood on the side of the road, stamping our feet, trying to get warm, silently casting blame on each other and hoping a driver would stop for us. I was pulled between my feelings of guilt toward Valerie and anger toward Leo for not understanding that we couldn't expect Valerie to be our chauffeur. Both of them were mad at me and hated each other.

"You should go back to Venice now, Leo. I'll stay with Valerie. I'm sure an Italian will be happy to help us with the car if you're not here."

Leo and Valerie shook hands without speaking. Valerie turned away to examine the damage to the car, while Leo and I said good-bye. We hugged, and I could still sense the warmth of his body through the leather. I felt sad, as though something had stopped before it started. I watched him cross the road, the collar of his jacket turned up against the cold. A truck filled with chickens heading for Venice picked him up almost immediately. He waved casually, making the little squeezing hand sign that meant *ciao,* from the passenger seat. A week in Italy, and we were so Italian.

A few minutes later, a man driving alone in a red Alfa Romeo stopped and beckoned us to the car. Valerie and I climbed in. She sat in the front, leaving the cramped backseat position to me. "My Italian's better," she threw off by way of explanation. The man behind the wheel was wearing a trench coat with a plaid wool lining and beautiful driving gloves, dark tan leather and beige mesh cut out on the top, revealing flat black hairs. I had only seen men wearing driving gloves in foreign films. In stilted but correct English, our rescuer told us he was a count. He certainly could have played one in a movie. He was a dead ringer for Vittorio Gassman, I thought. In our literary Italian, we tried to make a joke about being like the narrator of Dante's *Inferno*—lost in the "*selva*

oscura," the "dark wood" in the middle of life in which the poet's journey begins. Naturally, the count knew the entire poem by heart. As
he recited the famous lines from the first canto, I tried to get Valerie's
attention, but she seemed lost in rapture. Where were we going? What
about the car? The few things we had bought in Venice were in the
trunk, which was wedged into the ditch. Would we get back to Paris in
time for classes? I wondered miserably as I gazed out the window. We
could have been anywhere, the count a Mafioso or a serial murderer on
the loose. Not a car passed. "How stupid can you be?" my father's voice
echoed across the ocean. The question, which took itself for an answer,
was becoming the leitmotif of the trip. It was only four in the afternoon, but it was rapidly growing darker. The count turned on his lights.

"Signorine," the count interrupted himself, moving seamlessly
from the sublime poetry to the prose at hand, inviting us to spend the
night at his house. It was Sunday, and too late to have the car repaired;
he would take care of everything the following day. The count lived on
the outskirts of Padua on the road to Vicenza, he told us. His wife was
still in Venice with their daughter, but the maid would make us something to eat and give us something to sleep in; we would each have a
room to ourselves. Valerie accepted for both of us. This sounded like a
total con job to me, but Valerie, who had told me she thought Leo was
a phony, seemed to believe the count was for real. After a short ride,
the count pulled up in front of what looked like a Renaissance palace.
A maid in uniform showed us to our rooms. Mine was at the top of the
stairs, Valerie's at the end of the hall near the bathroom. I fell asleep
under a huge white duvet, hoping Valerie was right about the count.

The next morning when I came downstairs, Valerie was sitting at
the kitchen table wearing a man's bathrobe over men's pajama bottoms,
a long white terry cloth robe that stood out against the terra-cotta tiles.
She looked very pleased with herself, the way she had when the count
was reciting Dante in the car. The maid was making fresh coffee. Bread
and butter were already on the table. I could hear the count's voice on
the telephone, alternately laughing ("due americane") and business-like
(something to do with "accidente"), making arrangements for the
"macchina" to be repaired and brought to a garage in town.

"What happened?" I asked, staring at the bathrobe. Valerie still wasn't talking to me; she wouldn't even look my way. I reviewed the evening we had spent together after arriving at the villa the night before, our supper of vegetable soup and cheese, the discussion over wine of the famous Giotto frescoes in Padua that we should be sure to see before we left. Did we know that Dante had stayed in Padua, and Petrarch had too? While we were bantering about literature and art, Valerie and the count must have been exchanging signals I had failed to pick up. Leo must have been wrong about her being lesbian. Could it have started in the car? That was why Valerie had seemed so unafraid. But when had they decided? I wondered about the count's wife, remembering Philippe's shrug when I asked about Anne. Maybe the contessa didn't mind either.

Later that morning, the count drove us into Padua. The damage to the car had been less extensive than it appeared. Fiats were sturdy, the mechanic explained, with a touch of national pride. The count insisted on paying for the repair, refusing the offer of my remaining traveler's checks, the pale blue currency of American dollars that had diminished dramatically with our Italian misadventures.

"An American father would do the same for my daughter," the count said, dispelling the ambiguity of the sleeping arrangements after the fact.

Valerie smiled. I hated her. Whatever had gone on between them, the count had preferred Valerie to me. I was jealous, of course, but there was more. I felt stupid. I had failed to grasp the story I was in while it was unfolding. This wasn't the first time I had found myself missing the cues. On the drive back to Paris, I pressed Valerie about the count, but she refused to reveal the secret of her night in the palazzo.

"The count was active in the Italian resistance during the war," was all she said, as if they had spent the night talking about politics, or Giotto.

When I play *No Sun in Venice*, on vinyl, as they say now, the music crackles literally because of the scratches, but the metaphor works too. I hear the riffs I've listened to hundreds of times, but the sound isn't perfect. Like memory, the tracks of the album are slightly warped. I will never love any music as much as the jazz on my first LPs, and certainly never on CDs, which, free of scratches, carry nothing but the sound of music. I recently had my turntable and amplifier repaired to play this record and others that hold my past. But when I heard the Quartet at the Café Carlyle in the early 1990s, I couldn't feel anything. I recognized the melodies in their polished performance, but the sounds that had made me quiver left me still—moored in the present of a middle-aged woman well beyond her jazz age. The album was commissioned in the late 1950s as the soundtrack for a movie called *One Never Knows*. You never know what is going to happen, the opposite of believing in consequences. Now, of course, when I've played most of my cards, everything in my life seems an effect of those consequences I longed to banish from my horizon.

Jean Seberg's Fingers

WHEN CLASSES RESUMED AFTER CHRISTMAS, we had entered the short, dark days of January. I seemed to be gaining weight, and my period was late. Where would I have an abortion, if I was pregnant? How would I pay? In *Breathless*, Jean Seberg's Patricia, thinking she might be pregnant, examines her face in the mirror and counts the future on her fingers with an enigmatic smile. She looks pleased with herself, confident in that self-contained American-girl way. As I counted the days, I kept sliding a finger up between my legs and rooting around hopefully every time I felt the slightest twinge, scanning my nails for that precious sliver of blood that would spell release from the nightmare.

I wrote to Leo telling him I was afraid I was "in trouble," as the girls in *True Confessions*, whose destinies had terrified me in junior high school, would miserably confess as they saw their dreams crumble. Unlike Patricia, who contemplated the possibility of pregnancy with a modern girl's equanimity bordering on indifference, I reverted to the scenarios of dread and punishment I had grown up with. My father would immediately follow a lecture about virginity with the specter of a paternity suit in which I would have no credibility, as a willing participant in my wretched fate. "Who would believe you?" he'd demand rhetorically, as if he had already taken the putative father of my unborn child to court.

In my letter I didn't exactly blame Leo for what had happened, but he understood the place I was assigning him in the story. He sent a long reply from Rome, exiting from the script: "I just can't accept the role of guy-who-knocks-up-girl-and-cuts-out. Maybe some think that fits. I'm not sorry I made love to you, but that it wrought unhappy consequences." So what did that mean? "What do you want me to do?" he asked at the end of the letter, as if he had no ideas of his own.

I asked him to send me some money before he left for Greece. The vacation in Italy had used up my emergency fund of traveler's checks. The next time I could expect money from my parents was for my birthday later in February. I hinted in my letter home that I'd like a large sum for my twenty-first birthday to replace the clothing stolen in Venice. I actually had no idea how much money an abortion in Paris would cost. Five hundred dollars was what I remembered from friends "in trouble" in New York. I had decided I would ask Philippe for a name and to lend me the money if necessary. At least he was a doctor.

"What do you want Leo to do?" Monique asked, one afternoon when she found me sobbing on my bed.

"I don't know. I can't believe I'm in this situation. It's such a cliché."

From the beginning Leo was on the move: we were parting, it sometimes seemed, even as we got together. The road itself was the romance. I couldn't go on his trip; he had made that clear. Was I even in love with him?

Early one morning, a few days after the "unhappy consequences" letter, I was sitting alone at the café next door to the Foyer staring at my *tartine beurrée* as it soaked up the hot chocolate. I knew the hot chocolate was fattening on top of the bread and butter, but what difference did that make if I was already pregnant? The patter of the *balayeurs,* the street cleaners, who were mainly African—tall, thin, black men in dark blue jumpsuits, sweeping the gutters with their brooms of twigs—caused me to look up. Through the plateglass window of the café I saw Leo standing under a chestnut tree on the boulevard. I could barely make out his silhouette in the still dark hours of the Parisian winter morning.

"You didn't think I'd come, did you, baby?" he asked, when he sat down. He had caught a ride with friends, he told me. They had driven all night, and it showed on his face behind the smile of triumph. He signaled the waiter, as though this were an ordinary morning.

The fact that Leo had come from Rome was the most romantic thing that anyone had ever done for me. It was almost worth getting pregnant, I thought fleetingly, as I watched him sip his *petit crème*.

"I have an eight o'clock class at the lycée."

Leo stood with me at the bus stop on the boulevard Saint-Michel, his arm around my shoulder. He kissed me good-bye and I climbed on the bus. As the 27 bus crossed the Seine at the Pont-Neuf, I suddenly felt that familiar tug low on my belly, then a tiny cramp. My body prickled with excitement. I had escaped again. It was like surviving the car crash in Italy, a shuddering excitement laced with guilt. I had gotten away with something, but I might still be punished, I felt, in the nervous recesses of my nice-girl soul.

We met at Chez Ali that night, the couscous restaurant where we had had dinner on our first date. I told Leo about getting my period. It's not my fault, I wanted to say. How could I have known that I was only late, not pregnant? I felt embarrassed that I had panicked. Leo smiled, clearly torn between exasperation and relief. He ordered another carafe of red wine and we had second helpings of couscous, too. Leo was leaving the next morning. From Italy, he would be heading for Greece, returning to Paris only in the spring. When we kissed good-bye in front of the Foyer, he seemed almost sad that we were parting again.

A few weeks later, Leo wrote a long letter from Athens. He had figured out our relationship, he said, and what I meant to him. When he saw me through the café window in Paris, he realized that he could leave Europe and make his journey in peace, knowing that someone— that is, me—would be waiting for him. "You're a Person, a Riverside

Drive, Jewish, Barnard, Penelope, one to whom I can write and tell of my odyssey." I was pleased that "Person" (capitalized) headed the list. But somehow, Leo hadn't seemed to notice that I had left New York too. I had moved out of Riverside Drive, and Barnard was behind me. As for Jewish Penelope, she didn't plan to wait for Odysseus, at least not past the summer. Naturally, I didn't say any of that, including the reminder that in the *Odyssey* Penelope and Odysseus were married. As long as I was waiting, I liked getting the letters.

Wars of Independence

THE ALGERIAN WAR OFFICIALLY ENDED in March, and April in Paris resembled the Paris of the song. The chestnut trees on the boulevard Saint-Michel near the Foyer and in the Luxembourg Gardens blossomed. The horizon suddenly brightened from gray to pink. Despite the signs of the new season, as the spring wore on, Leo kept moving farther east, delaying his return. There were no promises between Leo and me, no words of love. I was waiting without expectation. Neither of us had scripted a scenario that put us into a shared future, though neither of us was willing to let go of the thread of affection that connected our stories until this point—Americans in Paris, the accident in Venice, the pregnancy scare.

I was writing to Leo. I was also writing to David, who was following my adventures with characteristic ambivalence. In every letter he lectured me about the fallout in Paris from the Algerian war, the acts of terrorism and repression that punctuated daily life and that he concluded I hadn't noticed. "Very concerned for your apolitical frailty in the midst of *grèves* and *manifestations*: stay indoors," he wrote, demonstrating his mastery of the French political vocabulary he'd been reading about in *Partisan Review*—the strikes and mass demonstrations that had snarled traffic and filled the newspapers all through the long, dark, winter days.

After Sartre's apartment on the rue Bonaparte was blown up, David fretted that I didn't seem to care about the terrorism in the streets, the explosions orchestrated by the Organization of the Secret Army, known by its acronym, OAS. It would have been impossible not to hear the slogans chanted rhythmically at demonstrations—*OAS Assassins*—and to read the writing that covered the walls of the city: ALGÉRIE FRANÇAISE. It meant "Keep Algeria French" or "Peace in Algeria." I was for Algeria's independence, of course, but it was true that in my letters the struggle for independence I described was mine.

What did I want? The less I believed in Leo's return, the more I lobbied for David's arrival. Why couldn't he finish his master's essay in Paris? Maybe we could reinterpret our past failure, start over in Europe. David mistrusted my motives. He didn't believe that what I wanted was life with him. "I am really afraid that all you are hoping for is a way back," he wrote, as I sketched out the new plot for our future. I wasn't in love with him. I was just scared of being alone and I was in love with our past, now idealized. He kept taking my side of the argument against me, the one I had used during the breakup, about why I had to get away, be on my own—the desire for independence that on the long gray days in Paris I was almost ready to relinquish. I sometimes wondered if he had been seeing someone else, but hadn't gotten around to telling me. I couldn't blame him for that since we were supposed to be free, but despite the breakup I wanted David to feel that our attachment to each other was the main deal—that no one else really counted. As long as we were exchanging letters, I figured, our bond, like our history, was still alive—at least on paper.

David wanted a story told in the present tense. My letters were less about Paris, he complained, than about me, and the part of me that had chosen Paris over him: "I wish you would write me a letter of its own time and place, not of its past and future, so I can cram some reality into the formal idea of your being 'away,' and get rid, once and for all, of that Jean Seberg who keeps crawling into your clothes, if not your accent."

I wasn't ready to get rid of Jean Seberg.

Monique, who had given me a copy of *The Portuguese Letters* for my birthday, was skeptical about my penchant for epistolary romance and about American boys who couldn't get their writing done. She didn't see Leo as an improvement over David. She inscribed her warning on the flyleaf, the key words of the message highlighted in her newly acquired English. "Tell all the boys, 'fuck you' and think how wonderful it is to be twenty-one like the Portuguese nun and filled with passion." Being like the Portuguese nun was not what I had in mind when I imagined turning twenty-one in Paris, though saying fuck you "à tous les garçons" would have been a good place to start.

"What do you want to happen?" Monique asked one afternoon at the *salon de thé*, as she poured out the remainder of the dark tea.

Monique could not return to live in Tunisia; the rest of her family would soon join the general exodus of Jews out of North Africa, where life was becoming more and more difficult. She had to find a way to stay in France. My boyfriend problem seemed a luxury to her. So did my chance to return home.

My parents kept pressing me to say when I planned to return home after graduation from Middlebury. My contract with the lycée where I had been teaching English would expire at the end of the school year. How was I going to earn money? I had felt almost from my first day in Paris that I wanted to stay in France for a second year, and I had applied for a Fulbright teaching fellowship. I had learned that it was bad strategy to bring up possibilities for discord in advance. They would leap into the breach with a long list of counterarguments designed to quash my desire. I'd just drop the news of the fellowship casually when the time came, I decided, as if it had been offered to me without my trying—if, of course, I was lucky enough to be chosen.

It sometimes seemed that I did nothing but wait that year—for Leo to return, for David to change his mind, to hear about the fellowship, to finish my master's essay on *Les Liaisons Dangereuses* and graduate. I was attached to the mail like the wretched Portuguese nun whose lover failed to match her desires and never wrote back.

In the end, David never came to Paris. The way he saw it, we were like the lovers in his favorite French movie *Children of Paradise,* who lose one another in the streets of Paris, held back by crowds pulling in opposite directions. David chose his closing metaphors from *Children of Paradise* rather than *Breathless,* but in fact neither film turns out very well. Whatever the movie, David couldn't come over to where I was, and I couldn't go back.

"Je suis très indépendante, tu sais," Seberg says defiantly to Belmondo, when he tries to put the American girl in her place. I wanted to prove that I was very *indépendante.* The word now appeared in my letters home with the French spelling, as if I had lost mastery over English and confused the two languages.

The war in Algeria was winding down and *indépendance* was the order of the day. Something was ending along with colonial regimes: the regime of the *parents terribles.* In the meantime, with another year away from home, I started to feel braver. My letters became my bombs.

A Room of Her Own

I STARED AT THE EIFFEL Tower outside the window of the maid's room I had inherited from Valerie when she returned to the States, wishing for the next installment of my American-girl-in-Paris movie, which naturally meant a new boyfriend. Without him, there was no story. I might fancy myself a marquise in Laclos' eighteenth-century novel (played by sultry Jeanne Moreau in the updated movie version), but even she, especially she, as it turned out, needed a companion to execute her plans.

The seventh floors of bourgeois apartment buildings like my new home on rue de l'Université were originally conceived as servants' quarters, with a communal toilet and a bathroom for which you needed a key. At some point after the war, apartment owners who could no longer afford live-in maids decided to rent out the rooms at prices no maid could afford. Typically, a *chambre de bonne* had a small sink with running water—usually just cold—and enough space for a bed, a cupboard, and a small table. Students, especially foreign students, who were in no position to make any demands and who could be thrown out with no warning, were the ideal tenants for the minuscule rooms at the top.

The irony was not lost on me that I was back living in a maid's room, but at least it wasn't located within my parents' apartment, where in my last year of college I had fashioned a bedroom for myself out of the sliver of space designated for the putative maid who would live conveniently next to the kitchen. In Manhattan, I had a view of the Hudson River that almost made up for the cramped dimensions of the tiny enclosure, where David and I had spent many intense hours eating pizza in the dark and watching the lights on the George Washington Bridge. In the mornings, the empty, grease-stained pizza boxes in the garbage confirmed my mother's worst suspicions about the nature of our relationship.

The Eiffel Tower had replaced the bridge, but no one had replaced David.

Alone in a space of my own for the first time in my life, I entered into a fervor of unprecedented domestic activity. I housecleaned with a passion I couldn't explain. "Speaking of my room," I wrote home proudly, sketching a detailed floor plan, "you won't believe it, but *I*, N.L. Kipnis, have spent the past two weeks sewing, washing the floor (me!), cooking, ironing! My room looks wonderful. I miss Leo immensely. David thing more or less over. Tonight Monique and I see *Hamlet* with Jean-Louis Barrault at the Odéon."

Sewing by hand with huge stitches, I made rudimentary curtains and pillow covers. Curtains transformed an alcove into a closet. The kitchen table was also my desk. My metal trunk from summer camp served as seating for friends. Bullfighting posters from Spain on the wall, a lambskin throw rug from Tunisia, and flowers in empty Chianti bottles completed the look of classic 1950s bohemia. My cooking repertoire was limited since the windowsill doubled as refrigerator, but with my little blue camping stove, I turned out meals, sometimes warming prepared food from the expensive charcuterie around the corner, more often boiling pasta to save money.

September, when you lived in academic rhythms, had a way of making the summer seem attached to another incarnation. After trying to finish his master's essay on the little table in the maid's room, Leo had returned to New York. "You know, baby, I really could have stayed, been with you—but I had to *do* something," he wrote from the BOAC departure lounge at the airport, contemplating with dread his trip back home. For months, I would find notes scrawled on scraps of paper and hidden in the room. But "Kissing your face" and "Write me, baby!" mixed in with my underwear made me sad. I didn't want any more relationships by mail. My parents were correspondents enough for an entire novel. When I told them that Leo, the great expatriate, had returned to New York, they resumed their campaign to find out how soon—after the school year that hadn't even started—I would be coming home. Did I want help looking for a job? "Oh, I don't know if I'll ever come back," I answered flippantly. "Obviously, the person I marry will have a good deal to do with it." Only marrying would put an end to the discussion.

According to the terms of the pact we made in New York, they would fund my master's degree and supplement my ridiculous salary as a teaching assistant, in exchange for which I would write them weekly letters. Once I decided to remain in France for a second year, that bargain was over. My parents weren't required to send me dollars, and I wasn't obligated to carve slices from my pound of writer's flesh to pay my debt. Thanks to the Fulbright that had come through at the end of spring semester, I could afford not only my place in Paris, but also a room in Poitiers, where I had been assigned to teach—as well as the commute, just under three hours from Paris by train. The fellowship provided more than money, though. Radiating an aura of international prestige, it converted what my parents considered an irresponsible whim into a narrative that they, committed to the education plot that had structured their own lives as the children of immigrants, could not resist. The grant offered both sides an alibi. I would never have admitted it to my parents, who were baffled by my determination ("Why do you always have to want more?"), but I was relieved to have begun another legitimate school chapter—a fancy fellowship, not an iffy boyfriend.

I longed to stay, even if I could never quite say why. Everything was just so, well, you know, French, I'd end up babbling. Didn't they coin the phrase *je ne sais quoi* for what you couldn't quite define but whose evidence was palpable? I wanted something from France—that "I didn't know what"—something besides the marriage story playing in our local movie theater. What else was a nice Jewish girl circa 1962 supposed to do? Desperate to be on my own, I had slithered out from under my parents' roof without releasing myself from their expectations for me. Or mine, for that matter. The embarrassing fact was that I needed someone to stay with in order to feel independent—to break the bonds tying me to home, to the girl I was trying so hard to leave behind.

Released from the contract, I kept the epistolary connection out of habit and anxiety, revealing and concealing, telling too much and not enough. For every good daughter narrative, a secret bad-daughter subtext competed. I wrote letters because I was afraid not to. I was afraid to let go of the person my parents thought I was—and that I thought I was, too—despite my also knowing that trying to please them or believing they were right would inevitably lead to more unhappiness for me.

I was a daughterly rat in a maze of ambivalence. I couldn't figure out which way to go without getting stung and flung back on myself without a reward.

Yom Kippur on the Right Bank

EARLY THAT FALL, MONIQUE FELL in love with Alain, a young law student from North Africa. We met him at the Danton, a café on Saint-Germain where we often went for drinks after dinner during the Year of the Foyer, as we referred to the first year of our friendship. Monique quietly vanished into an erotic haze, despite the fact that she lived nearby, around the corner in a room like mine, only with less freedom—a rented room in the dark apartment of a *vieille dame*. After Alain, Monique was there and not there. On a good day, her example inspired me—maybe I would fall in love, too. Mainly I felt deserted by her in a city that barely was returning to life after the shuttered month of August.

The semester in Poitiers didn't begin until November. Despite the unread volumes of Proust's long novel (my summer project), I decided to make a trip to England—and while I was there, to get a diaphragm, even though I had no immediate plans for its use. After the scare with

Leo, I wanted to be prepared. There was no planning for what had just happened to Monique—*le coup de foudre*—the lightning bolt that struck her with full force, just like that.

Le planning familial, as I had already discovered, was still illegal in France. But England was different. I flew to London—student flights were cheaper than the ferry and train—and found a B&B in a row of shabby brick hotels off Gower Street that catered to students and young tourists who didn't mind exchanging comfort for the Bloomsbury location. The room was barely wide enough for the narrow bed and tiny night table, but I didn't expect to spend a lot of time studying the flowers on the wallpaper that seemed to have absorbed the distinctive odors of Full English Breakfast. I consulted the phonebook at the front desk, picked the name of a doctor in a nearby neighborhood, and made an appointment for the following morning. After a long hour flipping through old magazines in the waiting room, I finally saw the doctor, who informed me with a friendly smile that birth control ran counter to his beliefs: I had managed to find an ardent Catholic in a country of Anglicans.

I resumed my quest after breakfast the following day. This time, I considered only Jewish-sounding names. I elected Dr. Abraham Friedman. When I bought an underground ticket for Golders Green in North London, the agent behind the counter queried with a smirk, "Goldberg's Green?" I answered politely, "No, Golders Green," until I finally understood the success of my research. I had found not just a Jewish doctor, but an entire London neighborhood famous for its population of Jews.

Dr. Friedman was my first gynecologist. After measuring me for the diaphragm and inserting it inside me on the examining table, he asked me to stand up and walk around the room to make sure he had achieved the proper fit. I chatted with Dr. Friedman, as though I were not half undressed, about London Jews and the approaching High Holidays. On the long ride back to my hotel room, I contemplated the freedom I had just purchased with a kind of anxious joy.

WHEN I RETURNED TO PARIS, I found myself thinking about me and Jews, now forever associated with my powdery new diaphragm.

But it wasn't just the office visit with Dr. Friedman, which in retrospect seemed more and more peculiar. Alain was Jewish—Monique admitted that she could not have married someone who wasn't—and I began to wonder whether that mattered to me, beyond the parental hysteria that the very *idea* of marrying a non-Jew would invariably provoke. Living in Paris made me feel both more and less Jewish. Except for the neighborhood around the rue des Rosiers in the heart of the Marais, whose landmark was Goldenberg's (a New York–style deli), and Belleville, Jews were almost invisible in Paris. That absence of obvious signs of Jewish life made me feel strangely cut off from my upbringing, a severance I wished for, or so I thought most of the time.

My parents had both grown up in Orthodox Jewish families. When they were first married, they kept a kosher home for their parents, and because it was what they had grown up with. Little by little they drifted away from orthodoxy and down to the more relaxed practices of Reform Judaism. But they drew the line at Christmas trees and still held to the importance of The Holidays, which were always capitalized in their discourse. The Holidays produced an annual crisis over my attendance at Temple Israel.

"But I don't believe in God," I'd say every year, in my adolescent righteousness.

My mother offered the pavement compromise: to turn up (nicely dressed) outside the synagogue when services were over. That way her friends could see that her children were still in the family picture.

I accused her of hypocrisy. Didn't she demand complete honesty from us?

After a while, my mother gave up the battle, though the war continued. My father researched the location of synagogues in Paris.

Yom Kippur fell in early October that year. Monique and Alain persuaded me to accompany them to services. I wondered whether, translated into French, the experience made foreign, the holidays would feel different.

I walked with Monique and Alain, and Alain's cousin Bernard, whom I had met during the Year of the Foyer, to Kol Nidre services at Temple Victoire, the biggest synagogue in Paris, in the ninth arrondissement behind the Opéra, not far from the big department stores. So here was where the Jews were! They looked familiar, I thought, as we approached the crowd. Expensively dressed women and men—all in hats—talking about their summer vacation (the main topic of the *rentrée,* the return to social life that was almost a season itself). The Rothschilds' Rolls Royce was parked in front of the synagogue entrance on the rue de la Victoire, which was being patrolled by the police. At first, I wasn't absolutely sure what the gendarmes were protecting. I had not until then associated bombings with synagogues, but this was the fallout from all the unresolved issues of the Algerian war. Despite the bevy of uniformed police, in style the scene resembled Manhattan sidewalks on the High Holidays. I could read the letter home forming in my head. My parents would be surprised.

The crowds inside replicated those outside, groomed and guarded. Unused to the geography of Orthodox synagogues, I climbed the stairs with Monique to where the women were sitting in a crowd of their own. The women were chattering among themselves, oblivious to the chanting going on downstairs, where men draped in prayer shawls swayed back and forth, beating their breasts in atonement. In Sunday school, I had spent so much time protesting that I didn't believe in God that my knowledge of Hebrew was almost nonexistent. But I didn't need to understand the words of the chant: the body language of the breast-beating was clear.

I begged Monique to leave with me, but she had promised to meet Alain when services were over. After a while, I walked out by myself and headed straight for the metro. What made me think God would be more attractive in Paris? Was it about religion or about my parents? Being Jewish had defined me when I was growing up; so had being my parents' daughter. I wanted to be free (my mantra) and I was afraid of being cut off. I couldn't untie the knot.

"What a farce!" I wrote at the end of my letter that night, as though we were back arguing about Temple Israel. "It really doesn't mean anything to me." As usual, my worst battles were with myself.

Les Cousins

ALAIN AND HIS COUSIN BERNARD shared a large apartment in a nondescript neighborhood just below the hills of Montmartre. While they were still living in Tunisia, Alain's grandparents had bought the apartment both as an investment and as a hedge against their future dispossession, thinking that they might have to leave the country on short notice and that this space would give them a safe base in France. In the meantime, Alain had the keys.

The cousins celebrated getting the keys to the apartment with a *boum*—a dancing party. Alain's younger brother played DJ, changing the records on *le pick-up,* the tiny turntable essential to creating the right atmosphere, alternating twists with mambos, but, as the night wore on, playing more and more "slows," as they were called in French. Eventually, most of the couples had almost stopped in their tracks, draped over each other as if they lacked the strength to move. At one point, after being glued together during several slows in a row, Monique and Alain withdrew to one of the little bedrooms and bolted the door. I danced with Bernard a while longer. Bernard was sweet. We kissed briefly. The kisses, standard *boum* behavior, were sweet, too, if not irresistible. I wasn't sure about Bernard. He was French, I reasoned, in language at least—wasn't I tired of American boys?—and he was there. Not in New York, where David and Leo were, but in Paris, where I was alone.

Two days after the party, Monique knocked at the door of my maid's room. She had deep circles around her eyes and looked exhausted. "Alain and I have decided to be together," she said quickly, as if to get it over with. *Ensemble.* That word. Not a passing fancy, the real thing.

I wasn't completely surprised—I had seen them disappear into the bedroom together the night of the *boum*—but I was almost speechless with disappointment. Because of her parents, Monique had to maintain the fiction of the room she rented, but Alain was coming over that afternoon to help her move her things into the apartment.

"Aren't you even happy for me?" she asked, hurt by my silence.

"Of course, I'm happy for you," I said. "I just didn't expect it to happen so soon."

"You know, the night of the *boum*," Monique began, looking down. I knew what she was trying to tell me. She trailed off, weary from the effort to say without saying. We had been talking about sexual passion for a year, and now it had happened to her.

"It was just like the books," she said. "You know." Monique smiled mysteriously. Neither of us was ever specific, though we both knew what was supposed to happen, where and how, but that still never had for me. I envied Monique's new attachment, so I began to spend time with Bernard, who was feeling abandoned too.

Table conversation between Bernard and me tended to flounder, except when he talked to me about growing up Jewish in North Africa and about his family, which seemed oddly like mine minus the exotic location. I thought I might like his mother, Sophie, who sounded sensitive and intelligent.

Bernard was addicted to Baby-Foot, the popular table soccer game many big cafés had set up toward the back of the room. He claimed that the game was his way of unwinding after classes. Although I had never seen much evidence of heavy study activity, Bernard swore that he did nothing but study when we weren't together.

"I don't know about Bernard," I said to Monique, who was promoting the relationship so we could be two couples together.

She insisted that he was perfectly intelligent, just not a *littéraire* like us. As far as I could tell, Bernard read nothing but crime novels by San Antonio, the French version of Mickey Spillane. I couldn't help comparing him to my old boyfriends.

Monique accused me of succumbing to nostalgia. I was remembering only the good times.

"That's what nostalgia is," she said. "Selective memory."

With Alain and Bernard, I had entered another movie, *Les Cousins,* the first new wave film I had seen with David in New York. An earnest country cousin (Gérard Blain) comes to live with his cynical city cousin (Jean-Claude Brialy) in Paris. Both are law students. The country cousin studies all the time and writes letters home. The city cousin has affairs and never cracks a book. The country cousin falls in love with the city cousin's girlfriend. This piques the city cousin, who decides to prove to the country cousin that the girl can't be trusted, that she will always come back to him. To make his case, the city cousin takes the girl's hand—pulling her away from the country cousin—and he places her hand inside his shirt, open at the collar. Once the girl puts her hand on Jean-Claude Brialy's chest, it's all over. She melts into his caress. Love, Brialy smugly explains to a crestfallen Blain, is just a matter of skin.

Even David was impressed enough to grow his hair long and get a jacket like the one the sexy cousin wore. I started wondering about skin.

Virtue is rarely rewarded in nouvelle vague movies. The city cousin passes his exams; the country cousin fails his. I feared that Bernard was going to fail his exams, given his city cousin study habits. It worried me that he assumed he would be lucky like the city cousin in the movie, without a care in the world.

What fascinated me in *Les Cousins* was the moment of instant, melting turn-on, when the girl touches the city cousin's chest. I had never had that experience, certainly not with Bernard, so I probably should have bailed out of that movie plot right then. The truth was that I was working on sex with Bernard, just as I worked on my French. At least the two worked together. I was as determined to come as he was to make me come, and it annoyed both of us—competitively—that it happened for Monique so quickly.

I wanted Monique's orgasm.

Mediterranean in looks and personality, Bernard was dark, with curly hair and brown eyes. His body, graceful and muscular, looked as though it would be at home on the beach, where he had grown up playing volleyball on the sand, but bed was not the beach. Bed was more like boot camp. Bernard assured me that what I wanted would happen only if he rid me of all my bad habits (*le système américain*), my years of training as a demi-vierge. All those exquisite caresses had short-circuited my capacity for real pleasure, he said. His project was to make me come without touching any part of my body with his hands. (Bernard had not read D.H. Lawrence on the subject, but he was as doctrinaire.) No caresses until we got to the next stage. Bernard would position himself above me and, holding himself aloft athletically, move around inside me. This is going to take a long time, I sometimes thought, admiring his stamina, as the nights wore on. But what was the point of not being a virgin if you didn't come?

This single-minded focus on coming was different from evenings in my room with Leo, which we mainly spent talking; coming was not a topic of conversation. "It will happen," he'd say reassuringly, "you'll see." Finally, one Sunday afternoon, when I thought the thrusting would never end, it happened. Not the magic I had dreamed of, true, not the earth moving, but I had to admit there was something palpably new, a head-to-toe spasm, something like an inner release. We emerged from the bedroom with our announcement. Bernard has conquered the American girl's frigidity, compliments all around. Alain broke out the champagne. The cousins congratulated each other.

I lifted a glass—undeniably, something had happened—but I felt embarrassed, diminished somehow, in my own eyes. (Was this what caused Monique to look shattered?)

"I had no wish to enjoy," the Marquise de Merteuil explains to her partner in crime, when she narrates her sexual history. "I wanted to know." I was chagrined to discover that for me, like the Marquise, thus far the *idea* of coming had been more exciting than the act; even so, she seemed to have reached the enjoyment part rather quickly. Maybe it wasn't the act but the partner. Maybe I was in the wrong movie again. It was hard to know. In the meantime, I would go along with Bernard's sex program, keeping my skepticism about it to myself. I wouldn't fake frigidity (what the Marquise said was the best way to find out what she liked; that way no man could ever think he had power over her) or orgasm, but I would stop reporting.

Practicing sex as I practiced the piano when I lived at home, for every new sensation, I gave myself invisible gold stars like the ones my Viennese teacher used to paste on my music pages.

Le Foot

FAMILY WAS THE SUPREME VALUE for Alain and Bernard. In practice this meant Sunday lunch with Bernard's older brother in the suburbs. The four of us would take a train around eleven in the morning and arrive in time for the ritual of the *apéro*. Drinks were the only time the television wasn't turned on for the afternoon soccer game (*le foot*). Bernard was the star of this interval, since as a group we had little to say to each other beyond exchanging anecdotes about family members, none of whom I knew, and telling jokes. Sometimes I recognized the jokes as borscht belt stories I had heard growing up. Bernard told the stories well, and I smiled hearing the punch lines in translation, even though joke telling itself made me nervous, as though I was being dragged back into the very past I had come to France to escape. Not the Jews exactly, but the humor of adults who joked instead of talking. The culture of the punch line was, I

thought, so—the word bubbled up, that French word in English—
so *bourgeois*.

Albert's wife, Edith, spent most of her time shuttling back and
forth between the kitchen and the round dining room table to check
on the progress of the meal. Monique and I sometimes followed her,
miming a female solidarity we didn't remotely feel. Edith was pregnant
with twins and huge. It was hard to imagine all of them living together
in their one-bedroom apartment. Their first child, a six-year-old boy who
sat in front of the television whether it was turned on or not, playing with
his toy car and chanting "Vroom, vroom" as he revved its wheels, already
made the rooms shrink.

The first time I went to Sunday dinner with Bernard's family, I
picked up a roast chicken leg with my fingers. No one commented until
I started gnawing on the bone, as we did in my family, sucking the sweet
marrow out of the knobby end. Bernard looked at me askance, gesturing
for me to put the bone back on my plate. The line between mock horror
and genuine indignation was hard to distinguish. Before Bernard could
speak, Monique sensed the great Franco-American battle about to begin
and decided to take my side. She put down her knife and fork and started
to eat her chicken leg with her fingers, daring Bernard by her gesture to
say anything.

On the train back to Paris, Bernard couldn't resist. "In France one
doesn't eat with one's fingers, even *en famille*."

"And in America one doesn't spend the entire afternoon watching
television." That probably wasn't true, of course, except in my parents'
house where television itself was taboo, but I figured I'd make the point
about having to watch people watch a soccer match for two hours.

After the third visit to the suburbs, I told Bernard he had to choose
between me and *le foot*. He looked hurt.

"Say I have to take the train to Poitiers on Sundays. I have classes
Monday morning."

Bernard would never have admitted it, but my solution appealed to
him. He could be himself with his family, saved from my obvious expressions of boredom, without losing face.

By the time I started traveling to Poitiers, I had formed an attachment in Paris I needed but that I didn't fully understand myself. Bernard was—the word I kept tripping over—different. "The essential thing, though," I wrote, "is that I'm very happy and feeling far away from all things American."

On the other hand, I was teaching what I was feeling so far away from: things American.

A Fine Fly

FULBRIGHT TEACHING FELLOWS WERE EXPECTED to lecture on the history and geography of their home state. Without a book on the subject issued by the U.S. government that my father had found for me, and that clearly divided New York State into different geographic and economic regions (complete with maps), my course would have been a total fiasco. Instead, I would stand at the bottom of a small amphitheater and weekly hold forth before fifty or sixty master's students who took notes assiduously, as though I were an authority. This excited me. No one had ever written down what I said. I lectured about the importance of the Hudson River; the role it played in revolutionary history; and the strange fact that as an estuary, it flows in two directions: down from the Adirondacks and up from the Atlantic Ocean, from Manhattan.

The river of my ambivalence, in a word.

I loved my days in the medieval university town, "and when I'm there," I wrote, "everything is perfect. Little narrow streets, old churches, etc. I go everywhere on foot. My 'kids' (who are certainly older than I am), come to class with an astounding regularity." I was especially eloquent on the subject of Indians, their unfortunate fate in American history. The French, I knew, were always well disposed to groups like Indians they perceived as persecuted in America, and I shamelessly flattered their prejudices.

I quickly made two good friends among the students in my class at Poitiers, Thomas and Micheline Gauthier, who were completing their degrees in English. They had married when Micheline found herself pregnant in their first year at university. They named their son Fabrice after the charming hero of Stendhal's novel *The Charterhouse of Parma*—their favorite novel. Micheline's parents, who lived in Tours, an hour away, took care of their exquisite blond child while they finished school. I was surprised that Micheline had not had an abortion. She said she was lucky: her parents loved taking care of Fabrice. I tried to imagine the reaction of my parents, faced with the news of a pregnancy out of wedlock, as they liked to say. My mother had already warned me she had no intention of babysitting for grandchildren, if that was what I had in mind.

The Fulbright commission had provided me with a letter of introduction for Madame de Rosemonde, a tiny, elderly woman whose house was a short walk from the Poitiers train station and the university. When I arrived in town at the beginning of the fall term, she showed me a large square bedroom, twice the size and half the price of my maid's room in Paris, with a big window facing the street. The room was furnished with a chest of drawers, a double bed covered with an eiderdown quilt, and a large desk. A flowered, porcelain chamber pot was tucked away behind the door of the night table; it matched the pitcher and basin on the washstand.

A simple black crucifix hung on the wall directly over the bed.

My first night I contemplated the crucifix and the chamber pot uneasily. Both presented a novelty. I wasn't sure, and had failed to ask, whether the chamber pot was meant to be used. But at night it was so cold in the staircase and in the *cabinet* at the bottom of the stairs that necessity resolved the quandary. The crucifix posed a problem of a different order. I had never slept under a crucifix, and now this would be a regular feature of my life. I could have taken the cross down, I suppose, and put it back up when I returned to Paris. I could have explained my discomfort to Madame de Rosemonde, but what would I have said? It's not as though I didn't know France was a Catholic country. The crucifix, I concluded, was just a symbol, like the national flag, and it did not prevent me from sleeping.

Madame de Rosemonde, approaching eighty, had trouble walking and so her confessor, Father Anselme, came to the house once a week. He was tall and wore a cassock that looked rather elegant, I thought, even if I couldn't help thinking that it looked like a dress. He seemed quite sophisticated, though I had no point of comparison, of course, having never known a priest. I sometimes talked with him over the tea that Madame de Rosemonde served in the salon—about America, especially about President Kennedy. I cherished my conversations with Madame de Rosemonde and Father Anselme. I never mentioned that I was Jewish, but my ignorance about things Catholic no doubt gave me away.

One day Madame de Rosemonde reported one day that Father Anselme told her that I was "une fine mouche." A fine fly? As always, when confronted with a new expression, I pretended to know what it meant until I could look it up in the dictionary: shrewd, clever, the opposite of a ninny. I was pleased, even though shrewdness, according to the dictionary examples, could also shade into the less flattering zones of ruse.

No Tomorrow

As far as my parents knew, when I wasn't in Poitiers, I was living in my maid's room, which I always used as my return address. But in early December, I entrapped myself. I had requested my bankbook from the New York branch to be sent to Paris. When it didn't arrive, I asked my father to inquire. I thought he'd be pleased that I was taking care of money matters on my own. The officer had just mailed the bankbook, he told my father, in care of Bernard Alvarez, as per my instructions.

Not a very clever fly, after all.

The evidence unleashed my father's patriarchal zeal: I had "shacked up" with Bernard, and in a dangerous neighborhood (near Pigalle) to boot. The *appearance* of disgrace (my father pretended to give me the benefit of the doubt) was horrifying, enough to raise "suspicions which would scare even a liberal French father to say nothing of an English, German, North African, or any other kind of father." Looking to rise above our own particular relationship, he located the drama on an international stage, turning up the volume, in case I missed the point: "I will quit moralizing if you can get me a single expression of approval from any father of any nationality whatever who will condone in his daughter what you are doing in Paris," "doing in Paris" having been crossed out and replaced by "what you seem to have let yourself in for."

As usual, my father was both right and wrong. I had more or less "shacked up" with Bernard. Little by little, without quite intending to, I found myself spending more and more time at the cousins' apartment, only going to my room for the mail. It seemed lonely and pointless to heat up my dinner on the little Butagaz stove in my maid's room. True, the apartment was in a seedy neighborhood. But what his daughter had "let herself in for" was less timeless international epic than early 1960s student domestic.

The cousins' apartment, a fifth-floor walk-up without an elevator, was a warren of once separate small rooms that had been hurriedly assembled. This layout guaranteed a minimum of privacy, or a maximum of sharing, depending on your view of communal life. You could shut the bedroom doors, but to go anywhere in the apartment you were obliged to pass through a common room that someone always seemed to occupy. The toilet was located in a chilly cupboard-like space between the kitchen and the front door. No sooner did you sit down on the wooden seat and slide the bolt into the lock than a fight about how long to cook the pasta would break out in the kitchen, or the front doorbell would ring and five more cousins would joyously announce their arrival in time for dinner. Compared to the elegant duplex the French movie cousins enjoyed, we were living in a slum. But compared to the run-down hotel rooms of the Latin Quarter and the overpriced maids' rooms Monique and I had managed to find in much nicer neighborhoods, this five-room apartment was luxury and a piece of luck. The government had requisitioned all available apartments for the French citizens returning from Algeria; without a political connection there was little chance of finding anything at all.

The apartment's centerpiece was the green-tiled bathroom, a hint that the original owners had had dreams of grandeur for their uncertain future. They had designed a *salle de bains* with a double sink, a long tub, and a bidet. But the plans for remodeling had been interrupted when the owners ran out of cash. There was no running water in the tub, and only cold water in the sinks and bidet. The North African cousins were not deterred by this minor drawback. Adept at the *système D* (the art of improvisation), they installed extra-long hoses, which ran from the kitchen sink, where a gas-driven *chauffe-eau* produced hot water, to the bathroom; the hoses snaked their way through the living room and down a small hallway, finally reaching the tub. Of course, you couldn't be in any kind of hurry for your bath, and the hot water had a way of cooling off by the time it had filled the tub, but still, the bathroom was *inside* the apartment, and that was a thrill in itself. How many people did I know who lived *with* a bathroom? Not to mention a bidet.

Bernard and I spent a lot of time in the bathroom. We had our best conversations in the peaceful green-tiled room, separated from the traffic in the apartment. Filling the tub itself was such a production that not to take full advantage of having the hot water didn't make sense. Once you had climbed over the steep edge of the tub and lowered yourself into its enameled length, there was a distinct sense of well-being. The sound of the *chauffe-eau* turning on with a kind of deep chug promising future warmth always gave me a small frisson of pleasure that matched the little blue flame, like the sound of pipes clanking when the heat first comes on in Manhattan apartments in early fall. One of us would sit on the bidet and smoke while the other took a bath. Then we'd switch. We didn't mind sharing the water. Alone in the bathroom, we speculated about what would happen the following year when I no longer had my fellowship. Maybe the lycée would take me back. The *directrice* had told me to come and see her if I decided to stay on in Paris.

I asked Bernard what he would do if he didn't pass the exams. He had already failed once. If he failed again, he would have to do his military service.

"Maybe I'll be assigned to Tahiti," he said, dripping water down my back. "And you could teach English to the natives." It wasn't completely a joke. Thomas, my friend from Poitiers, had just been posted to Tahiti, where he would be teaching French. Micheline and Fabrice were planning to accompany him.

I imagined the notice in the *Barnard Alumnae Magazine*. "Nancy Kipnis has married Bernard Alvarez. She will be living in Tahiti while Bernard completes his military service. Nancy looks forward to hearing from all alums living in the area." Right, I could start a Barnard club in Polynesia. *South Pacific.* "Some Enchanted Evening." I knew the song by heart. My father loved to croon the words as he stood at the edge of the living room, even when we begged him to stop.

My FATHER MOVED IN HIS brief from questions of struggle between the generations to even loftier zones of universal value and morality. True independence, which was always the pole around which my struggle for freedom revolved, was about consequences. My sleeping arrangements seemed to suggest that I had missed the essential lesson of my upbringing: living "as if there is a tomorrow, because there is one. I'm not suggesting a cloistered existence, but surely between it and libertinism there is an area of human satisfaction and gratification that need not stifle the most restless spirit." My father signed his letter, "As ever (because you can't change it), D" (*ad* crossed out).

Was there or wasn't there a tomorrow?

I was tempted to tell my father about a famous eighteenth-century story titled "No Tomorrow," in which a married woman has a one-night stand, experiences great pleasure, and does not get punished for it. But I figured that would just make his case. I was neither married nor a French countess.

The only way I could put an end to the criticism of my libertine tendencies was to say that things had become serious between Bernard and me. (That was how my parents always framed relationship queries: Is it "serious"?) In fact, I hinted, we were thinking about getting married. Thinking about it wasn't the same as having a concrete plan, of course, but the idea of marriage had entered our conversations in part because Alain and Monique had decided to marry when Alain finished his degree, and in part because it seemed a way to deal with the uncertainty of the future, to curb the anxiety of the drift. Bernard and I had become engaged, for lack of a better word, despite the financial impossibility of translating that word into action. My father had not been entirely wrong about the tomorrow problem.

Sometimes, when I returned to Paris from my weekly trip to Poitiers, often alone in a compartment on the beautiful high-speed train, I'd try to sort out my feelings. I loved the teaching; I loved speaking French; I loved being away from home. Did I also love Bernard? Going to Tunisia was taking a public step forward in the marriage plot, but was that what I wanted, or was I just copying Monique and Alain? They were happily sliding into domestic bliss as if it were their destiny. What was wrong with me? It was true that marrying Bernard would guarantee that I'd never live in America. I liked that idea, but it was less clear that hooking my fate to Bernard's would also mean that I wanted to make my life with him the way Monique had already done with Alain. Fighting for my right to marry him against my parents' wishes had moved me into a narrative turn I wasn't sure I was ready for, even if I refused to give ground. But I couldn't figure out what to put in its place, another kind of story. And besides, we had bought our tickets for Tunisia.

Bernard wanted to show me where in North Africa he had grown up and introduce me to his family. Everyone was curious about the American girl. I wasn't sure I was ready to meet the parents, but refusing seemed harder than accepting. I wanted to see the city I had read about in my high-school Latin class: Carthage.

On the eve of my trip to Tunisia, I described my involvement with Bernard, defining his appeal: "Outwardly, Bernard seems entirely different from me and all the other boys I've been with, but underneath we are very much the same. We get along perfectly—almost—and he is very good for me in all ways." Unfortunately, through the hedge of *almost*, and, worse yet, by giving an example of what in the relationship was less than perfect, I had opened the door to my father's prosecutorial scrutiny. I also made the mistake of mentioning that Bernard liked to tease me (my gnawing on the chicken leg had become one of his favorite digs) when he thought I was acting "American"; whatever was wrong with me derived from that.

Bernard also thought I was too complicated. "Complicated" was code to mean that I argued about everything, rather than accepting his views. I was bothered, I admit, by a kind of exaggerated masculinity that I tried to explain in the same way, by cultural difference; I chalked Bernard's swagger up to his North African upbringing, which reinforced the standard French line. *Vive la différence* seemed to mean that men were right and women should wear sexy underwear. "The main difference," I wrote to Judy, a Barnard classmate who had married in our senior year, "is that here things are clearly MALE-FEMALE—with no possibility of doubt—and *I* am the inferior being. I hesitate to go into details because I am quite confused about my feelings at this moment, and anything I write now will inevitably be contradicted tomorrow." I didn't say anything about my confusion to my parents. Nor could I tell them (or Judy, for that matter) about Bernard's sexual program for correcting my truly worst American-girl habits. And as always, what I couldn't possibly say, let alone admit fully to myself, ended by tripping me up.

In a surprising burst of literary criticism, my father decided to analyze the portrait of Bernard I had painted in my letter. Promising that he would not throw a tantrum, but that he couldn't help acting like a lawyer, he performed an *explication de texte* of my letter in a two-page brief, handwritten on onionskin legal paper with a red rule. His handwriting, like his logic, couldn't have been clearer and he crossed out only one word.

> *I'm only going to take up those items, which you disclosed, which I deem of substantial significance. I am concerned about his making fun of you. This is out and out subliminal ["disguised" crossed out] hostility and aggression, vis à vis you. It's*

*close to a form of bullying. It is a not unknown phenomenon
and in my amateur analysis reflects a not so good adjustment.
As to masculinity, "he likes to think he dominates me," is of a
piece with my first comments. Why should a person want to
dominate another? Respect, it seems to me, would be a better
objective. Temperament is a form of self-indulgence.*

*As to playing at being inflexible—that's all right for a
Nazi, but not for a husband or father. Since you imply that the
inflexibility is "to impress," is it not indicative of some sort
of insecurity?*

After working his way through all the other problems—the army,
school, financial dependence on his parents—my father concluded with
a conciliatory note: "Please believe me, I would love to be able to say, Go
ahead—get married—love will cancel out the minus factors. I just can't
do it on the basis of what you have told us."

Finally, abandoning the psychological, and in an attempt to get a
complete picture of the material details (the real "minus factors"), my
father attached a questionnaire at the bottom of the letter for me to
detach (*TEAR HERE*) on the dotted line and return:

1. *Do you have a definite grant for next year and where?*
2. *How old is Bernard and how many more years of school
   does he have to complete?*
3. *How much army service does Bernard have and when?*
4. *Are you definitely returning to your room in June?*
5. *Are you planning to "visit" New York and how will you
   finance it?*

I dutifully filled out the questionnaire about Bernard and mailed
it to my father in New York. The only unambiguous information I could
offer was Bernard's age: the same as mine, twenty-two.

I had opened the door a crack to my father's skepticism by airing
my anxieties. But I didn't expect him to fling the door wide open. The
skill of his "amateur analysis," as he styled it, unnerved me. In some ways,

Bernard's macho teasing was familiar—a variant of David's parrying—and usually silly. And it was the other side of extreme tenderness, kisses on the eyelids at night, smooth caresses on my forehead. He called me his *petit cornichon*, a nickname inspired by his view of my nose as a pickle. (Granted, not exactly flattering, but endearing nonetheless. Maybe I should have mentioned that in my letter.)

Still, my father's question irked me. "Why should a person want to dominate another?" It was a fair enough concern, if you removed the hyperbole of "Nazi." The letters stood out starkly on the page. Of course, I thought, as I mulled over my unwritten response, he never noticed how he tried to dominate me. What was this indictment of my judgment, if not an elaborate form of bullying? Turning my words against me. It was for my own good, as he liked to say, justifying his exercise of authority when my sister and I were growing up. "It's for your health and welfare." I knew that's how he would answer the charge of authoritarianism. The welfare department knew no borders.

My father seemed not to notice how completely, in his marriage, my mother dominated him; at least he didn't act as if he suffered from it. Maybe "Nazi" was the unconscious expression of his private pain. I hated my mother's spousal superiority. It was wrong, I thought, for a wife to dominate her husband. In return, I was determined never to do that to mine. But when it came right down to it, I never liked being bossed around. Even as a joke. That part my father had right.

Easter in Tunisia

BERNARD AND I WENT FOR long walks along the beach on the outskirts of Tunis at night and during the day sat in cafés along the main drag, smoking and soaking up the sun.

"I'm late," I told Bernard one afternoon, as we returned to his parents' apartment.

"How late?"

"At least a week," I said, fingering the hand of Fatma, the amulet against the evil eye I had picked up on my first excursion into the bazaar.

"We'll get married," Bernard said with a comfortable smile, holding me close to him to confirm his enthusiasm. "You could live here while I do my military service."

"I don't think so," I said slowly, releasing myself from the protective circle of his arm. "I'm not ready."

Bernard's smile faded. I knew he was disappointed. I also knew that the prospect of having a child with Bernard in Tunis terrified me as much as it had with Leo in Paris.

When two weeks had gone by, Bernard told his mother that we were worried.

"What do you want to do?" Sophie asked me over tea in her immaculate kitchen.

"Anything to get my period," I said with sudden vehemence, looking at the palm trees outside the window as though they threatened my existence.

"Are you sure?" she asked, squeezing my hand. "I wouldn't mind being a young grandmother while Bernard does his military service."

I didn't want to live in Tunisia, and it wasn't just the camels. True, I was enraptured by the scent of jasmine and orange blossoms, the pine nuts soaking in mint tea, and the shopping bargains to be had in the Souk. My arms were covered with bangles that tinkled with every gesture. The languor of the climate was seductive, but what would I do in a small provincial city? The women were cordoned off into their own world of domestic concerns. I could sense how restless Sophie was now that her children were grown, how much a grandchild would mean to her, and I was touched that faced with my distress, she quietly arranged for me to get a series of hormone injections to bring on my period; her brother owned a pharmacy in town.

Bernard and I passed through a curtain of beads to a small storeroom in the back of the pharmacy. His uncle told me to lift my skirt in a tone that made it sound as though that was how I had gotten into trouble in the first place. I had always dreaded injections, but as I stood there gripping the counter, I welcomed the pain of the thick fluid moving slowly into my muscles. I would have tolerated even more if it meant bringing on my period. Afterward, we sat for a while and smoked until I was ready to go back to Bernard's family. Every day for the next week, I weighed myself at the pharmacy and moved the steel weights to the right. Three more shots and we would make the next decision.

At the house, we would sit for hours, it seemed, at the dining room table. I prayed that this crisis would be like the last time with Leo, a little more than a year ago, when the pregnancy turned out to be a combination of pasta and anxiety. Now that overly sweet, sticky pastry I didn't even like. Crushed almond paste. Colored jellies. Glossy, fried dough. One morning I noticed a tiny spot of blood on my underpants. When nothing followed the brownish dot, we made an appointment with a gynecologist who was a friend of the pharmacist. Dr. Habib examined me and said that the injections had caused the egg to fall, but that my tubes were blocked. At least that's what I thought he said, translating through my anxiety.

"So I'm not pregnant?" He looked at me incredulously for not using the diaphragm just because Bernard didn't like the idea of it.

The doctor said he couldn't tell me that without further examination in his clinic.

Maybe I was still pregnant; maybe we were speaking about an abortion, only in code. This was a country in which you could never be sure what was going on; so much was wrapped in decorum and unsaids.

The next morning Bernard's mother drove us to the clinic thirty minutes away from the center of the city. It appeared to be a maternity clinic, since most of the patients I saw had huge bellies. The doctor ushered me into a big room with a high ceiling and bright lights. I climbed up on the examining table and placed my legs in the stirrups.

Someone took my arm and inserted a drip. The lights started to fade. I felt a rapid shudder of peace.

"MAKE THEM STOP CRYING," I could hear myself saying.

We must have been on the floor for newborns, who were screaming their tiny lungs out down the hall. I was propped up in bed with an ice pack on my stomach and thick layers of cotton pads between my legs. Bernard was holding my hand, gazing at me sweetly. His mother was there too.

"You're fine," she said, with a kind expression on her face. "The doctor just cleaned you out."

The next morning the three of us returned to Tunis.

Cleaned out, I thought, like Valerie's car in Venice.

Dog Days

LES PARENTS TERRIBLES STARTED PRESSING me to explain my living arrangements. We made a phone date. Transatlantic calls required elaborate planning and timing. You had to determine the time first by letter or, more urgently, by telegram. Then you had to go to a post office that could handle the calls. After you left your number at the main desk, you sat down to wait your turn until a booth came free. It was so expensive to talk for even a few minutes that we avoided calls whenever possible, especially as I tended to cry, which prolonged the conversation. Still, my parents were determined to clarify the status of my relationship with Bernard.

Serious or not serious?

"Look, doll," my father began, "we're just trying to understand what you feel." I could hear my mother making sarcastic comments in the background. My father handled matters when things seemed to have spiraled out of control. The term of endearment marked his willingness to hear my side of things.

"I don't know."

"You're living with the guy, aren't you?"

How could I explain that I was living with Bernard precisely in order to find out what I felt about him? I knew that would fall under the category of experimenting, one of my biggest crimes in my parents' eyes, along with not thinking about consequences.

I looked out at the other booths and wondered what conversations were going on behind their closed doors. I lit a cigarette and opened the door.

"For the moment I want to be with Bernard," I said. "I explained that in my letter."

I squashed the cigarette butt under my foot and shut the door to the booth again. I could tell my father was trying to calculate the cost of the phone call along with my feelings.

"Well, don't make any decisions until we come to Paris," he finally said.

My ear was starting to sweat.

"And don't tell any of our friends about your living arrangements."

I told him they already knew. I wasn't addicted to the truth. But I figured they would find out sooner or later. I started to tell my father that Bernard's parents thought I was great, but he had stopped listening.

My father followed up on the theme of the phone conversation in his next letter. "I don't give one shit what Bernard's parents' viewpoint is," he wrote, never losing the thread. He fantasized the reactions of friends and even strangers, not just in Paris but also in New York. People coming up to him in the street and shaking their heads in sympathy, then going off to gloat.

> *One thing is sickeningly clear. Now all I am waiting for are expressions of pity or consolation. Try to recall that Philippe and Anne are our friends, not yours. You talk about being happy for the first time etc. etc. Well, bully for you! Did you ever give a fleeting moment's thought to our happiness?*

You wish to marry—go ahead. But don't talk to us about marriage and prospective fornication for at least 3½ years in the same breath.

The heat wave of July 1963 made Paris as hot as New York ever gets in summer. The French call the miserable, humid, sticky weather *la canicule*—dog days. They always seem surprised when the dog days arrive. The French don't believe in air-conditioning because despite the evidence, they maintain that it doesn't really get hot in the summer.

My parents flew to France, and I went to their cool room in the Castiglione, a small, elegant hotel on the Faubourg Saint-Honoré. I'd been dreading this moment and, in a strange way, longing for it, too. The letters were brutal. I hated being on trial. I hated the language of moral sanction they both indulged in: we cannot *condone* your situation. Fornication. *Prospective* fornication.

So there they were, my mother and father, smaller than in their letters but more alive too. My father dapper in a fresh, light blue seersucker suit, my mother tan from weeks of tennis and bursting with energy for the social whirl with their old friends in Paris. In their division of emotional labor, my father composed the prose, and my mother handled the face-to-face confrontations. My mother turned to me and said with the tone of resigned exasperation she had perfected for dealing with my crises: "Are you sure you really want to marry this boy?"

There were no words. Just tears. I could not stop crying. No, I didn't want to marry him; I didn't want to go to Tunisia with them; I didn't want to hurt him; I didn't know how to get out of this. But mainly, I was sobbing American *jeune fille* tears.

Bernard and I had both feared the arrival of my parents, their opposition and resistance. We had hoped that when they traveled with me to Tunisia that summer, the two families would embrace. We knew there would be difficulties to resolve, especially financial ones, but neither of us had imagined the collapse of our future through the prick of the single question from my mother: "Do you really want to marry this boy?" Bernard was hurt and baffled by my withdrawal, but he consoled himself by mocking the materialist views of my American parents, for whom he was not in economic terms "un parti," as he wrote to Monique and Alain. My rejection came for Bernard on the heels of failed exams, the certainty of the army, and the misery of a sunburn from days spent stretched out on the beach as he waited for me in Tunisia.

I felt guilty, but at least I had written a letter and not telegraphed an adieu, as my parents had urged me to do. "Get it over with," my mother said, echoing my silent thoughts. "No matter how you say it, he's going to feel hurt." I compromised, sending a telegram saying I wasn't coming to Tunisia with my parents after all, and that a letter would follow. I was extremely fond of him, I said in the letter, but it wasn't a great passion and I wanted to experience that. He deserved better. I took the blame on myself, my famous complications. I hoped he wouldn't have too many regrets. I asked him to forgive me.

In Tours that July, my friend Nicole married Laurent, the French engineer she had become engaged to while she was still at Barnard. It was my first church wedding. The bridesmaids wore matching dresses: sleeveless pink linen sheaths with pumps dyed to match and white gloves that covered the wrist (*très* Jackie). In the wedding pictures, we all primly carry missals in our left hands and hold our partners' arms. With my hair teased high in a beehive, I walked down the aisle with Guy Dubosc, one of the groom's friends; he was short and blond and not for me. Nicole wore a long white dress and a lace mantilla; she carried white lilies. Laurent had finished his degree; his future was assured and predictable.

I envied Nicole's happiness.

"Everybody who is anybody is married with ten children," I wrote to Judy, after seeing my news reported in the *Barnard Alumnae Magazine* by a classmate who had passed through Paris. "And I feel strange." All my close friends had married; some were pregnant. I had just exited from my own bridal fantasy script, and all it had taken was my mother's "Do you really want to marry this boy?" to utter the "no" that had been forming in me but that I couldn't admit to myself. Why did what seemed simple for them seem so difficult for me?

"Do you think I'm immoral?" I asked Judy, when I wrote to tell her about breaking up with Bernard. The pleasure we had in bed seemed like an introduction to a story that had never progressed, I said.

After the emotional reconciliation with my parents, I regressed to, if I had ever left, dependent-child mode. Since ending the relationship with Bernard, I had been unable to decide anything. What didn't I want, the marriage or the boy? When my parents offered to take me with them on their vacation, I renounced my principles of independence and tagged along, weeping periodically in the backseat of their rental car. They were driving to the French Pyrenees and across the border into Spain. It was a minor consolation to be out of Paris in August, where you felt like a second-class citizen or worse, a tourist, if you were still in town—which you were. We stopped in France for the weekend at the little beach town of Collioure, along the Côte Vermeil.

When she couldn't find a tennis partner, my mother became absorbed by chess, which I taught her to play, having just learned myself from Thomas and Micheline, the student friends I had made at Poitiers. From her very first game, my mother beat me because she couldn't help being good at everything, especially if it was a game. I lacked both the talent and the emotional juice to compete seriously; I was resigned always to lose to her. There was actually a kind of comfort in surrendering to her power—at least, temporarily—and to the family frame. While the girls, as my father referred to my mother and me in his diary, went shopping and to the beauty parlor, my father looked for a place to buy the *New York Herald Tribune*.

One rainy day at Argelès-sur-Mer, a beautiful sandy beach surrounded by pine trees in southwest France not far from the Spanish border, my mother decided I needed a dress for dinner at the hotel. She bought a tablecloth of local black and white Catalan fabric and cut it into a sheath, sewing it by hand, fitting it on me in the hotel room. On the first try, the armholes were so high that I couldn't lower my arms, and the neck was so tight I could barely breathe. Seeing me imprisoned by her handiwork reminded my mother of a joke about garment district Jews, which made her laugh so hard she could barely tell it. I stood choking in the dress as my mother interrupted herself to tell the story, overcome with hilarity in anticipation of the punch line.

My mother couldn't stop laughing; then my father started, and finally, I gave in. The three of us fell out on the bed, almost in tears. I hated myself for laughing with them—not only because the joke was cruel, but also because laughing at the punch line of a story that belonged to them made me feel that I still hadn't left home.

That night, I wore the dress to dinner. It fit perfectly. The maître d' gave both of the girls a rose.

I LOOK AT THE PICTURE taken by a Paris street photographer that I had sent my parents as a down payment on the face-to-face encounter— still months off—that they would be having with Bernard, when we all went to North Africa. The photographer has stopped us (we're such an attractive couple—engaged?—we must want a picture of ourselves) and here we are posing near the Place de l'Opéra, not far from American Express, where I had gone to buy traveler's checks. Bernard is clearly producing his picture smile, though smiling is something that comes easily to him—it's his best feature—but I am smiling, too. The photographer must have trotted out his best lines, or maybe I really was happy.

That day Bernard had dressed for an interview at the firm of a friend of his father's in case he didn't pass his exams. He is wearing a three-piece suit, and his *collier*, the standard-issue student beard that connects the jaw line to the mustache, looks recently trimmed. I'm wearing pumps and sheer stockings, a gray suede coat with raglan sleeves my mother had bought for me on one of her shopping sprees. She bought the same one for herself in beige. I wanted to look older, my mother wanted to look younger—it was a moment in history when that meshing of the generations worked, in clothing, at least. In a snapshot of my parents taken in front of the Opéra by one of their friends, my mother and father strike almost the identical pose.

In the picture, Bernard and I do not appear to be as ill suited to each other as we in fact were.

Dancing in Barcelona

FOR YEARS, WHEN I WAS growing up, I fantasized that over the summer I would become, as if by magic, the person I always wanted to be when school started again: thin, tan, popular, with long hair. Then, I would meet someone. That September in Paris I was thin and tan and my hair had grown as long as it ever would, grazing the tops of my shoulders.

I was waiting to see whether Jonathan Alterman, whom I had met during the vacation with my parents, would turn up in Paris as he had promised.

A bipolar shopper, my mother alternated between extravagance and extreme frugality. On our first day in Barcelona, we headed for a wholesale leather shop on the Ramblas my parents had discovered on an earlier trip. This was bargain time, literally in a basement. While my mother and I tried on the black leather skirts and vests that hung in multiples along the movable racks, my father struck up a conversation with our counterparts in the store, the Altermans: Jewish, middle-class, from Maplewood, New Jersey, traveling with their adult child. Jonathan Alterman and I entered into a parallel exchange. Although he was already married and separated, as I rapidly learned (Jonathan was working in Argentina for the U.S. government while his two sons were living in the States with his wife), he was as stuck as I was in the kid role. We both stood around awkwardly, shifting weight from one foot to the other, checking each other out and rolling our eyes at various parental exclamations. Not only were we all staying at the same hotel, the Ritz, but his parents and mine knew a lot of the same people, the predictable map of Jewish geography. My mother and I chose exactly the same knee-length black leather skirt. My father paid for the skirts, peeling off several traveler's checks. Jonathan's parents, having progressed to grandparent condition, bought leather jackets for his boys. We all ate lunch at a place famous for its tapas that had been recommended by the hotel concierge.

The next day Jonathan and I met in the lobby of the Ritz at 9 PM—a little early by Barcelona standards, but after all we both had grown up eating dinner at 6:30. (My father noted in his diary without comment that Jonathan had called to invite me to dinner. He seemed unfazed by the fact that Jonathan wasn't divorced yet, or perturbed by the idea of Argentina after Tunisia. At least Alterman was earning a living.) Over wine we talked about Gaudí's buildings, his unfinished masterwork, the Sagrada Familia, and Jonathan's family crisis. He was on the verge of divorce and felt sad being separated from his blue-eyed, blond-haired boys, aged four and six, neither of whom looked remotely like him. Jonathan wore thick, tortoiseshell owlish glasses, which I didn't mind too much, even though he was the first man I'd ever gone out with who wore glasses. He was tall, heavyset, with regular features, a good nose and chin (I could never resist the genetic inventory for prospective children). He might have been handsome, I calculated, if he were thinner. But he wasn't—thinner, that is. He was also the first man with children I had ever dated, if this was a date, which it seemed to be.

We were moving smoothly across the dance floor of the hotel restaurant following the rhythm of old American tunes. I felt a slight pressure in the small of my back as Jonathan guided me gracefully, so expertly that I couldn't help wondering whether he had taken ballroom dancing lessons. There was something to be said for a man who could dance well. Wasn't that one of the secrets of my parents' marriage? David, on principle, didn't dance, and in Paris, Bernard, who was an excellent partner, danced the mambo and the cha-cha (you couldn't really count the slow). Jonathan pulled me in closer, romantically, as though for him we were people in a musical, and he whispered, movie-like, holding me tight and squeezing my hand, "I knew it would be like this." It was true that we moved well together.

The late summer encounter with Jonathan seemed to reassure my parents that I wasn't a lost cause. It was as though his familiarity—they didn't know his parents but they might have—consolidated the rapprochement the vacation had brought about. They could recognize me as their daughter again, and, in the moment, I was willing, or at least lonely enough, to be reclaimed.

Back in Paris, I wondered about Jonathan, whether I'd see him again. I wondered almost peacefully since the idea of him in my life seemed more like a transition, a pause in the downward spiral caused by the breakup with Bernard, than like the marker of a new departure. Dancing in the dark offered an unexpected, even comedic coda to the little melodrama of betrayal in which I had played so shabby a part. I couldn't help feeling that whatever happened with Jonathan would be yet another variation on the theme of my man-to-man drift. I could not see what good might come to me from following his star (his established career) rather than Bernard's flops, beyond a dollop of prestige.

And yet despite my doubts about a future with Jonathan, I suspected that I would end up sleeping with him if he came to Paris as promised, on his way back to South America. I was embarrassed in my own eyes by the feeling of inevitability that a new liaison might be starting in the wake of the old one barely over. And yet I found myself deciding to find a doctor who would give me a prescription for the birth control pill, since if I lacked the will to say no, I had learned enough from the experience with Bernard to know I couldn't risk putting myself in danger again so soon.

ᴊALL FORMS OF CONTRACEPTION HAD been banned in France since 1920, but a few brave doctors had been willing to run the risk of breaking the law. I had read about a doctor who had been involved in making the pill available to women in France through *le planning familial*. Dr. Pierre Hirsch was a famous gynecologist and an expert on birth control. Jewish too, I figured, judging by his name, and I made an appointment to get a prescription.

This was the first time I had been to a gynecologist in France. Dr. Hirsch's office was located in an elegant building on the boulevard Saint-Germain. When I rang the bell, a maid in uniform came to the door and ushered me into the large foyer of what appeared to be a huge apartment. Unlike American doctors, who had deliberately impersonal waiting rooms, French doctors almost always practiced in residential apartments, often their own. The living room in which patients waited their turn to see Dr. Hirsch was *his* living room, with comfortable furniture, real paintings, and fresh-cut flowers. It was quiet, so quiet that I began to wonder whether he lived alone, whether there was a Madame Hirsch and little ones, not to mention other patients. The taste and expensiveness of it all were intimidating, raising my already high anxiety about gynecological examinations. But after a few minutes, the door to Dr. Hirsch's office opened, and he motioned me to cross the threshold. As I sat across from him and gazed at the glass-enclosed, built-in bookcases behind the Louis XV desk and answered questions about my periods and how often I had sex, I wondered about which books he read and which were for show.

Dr. Hirsch led me to the door of a separate room, where I removed my clothing, hopped on the cold examination table, and waited anxiously for him to come in. I hoped the experience wouldn't be as creepy as my London gynecological excursion, and I was at first uneasy at being alone with this impeccably tailored, over-six-foot tall French doctor—the tallest man in France I had ever seen. If he had been wearing a white coat, it might have felt more normal for me to undressed. My strategy for coping was to pretend that it didn't faze me to be stretched out naked on the table, even though I never stopped worrying about every exposed part of my body. While Dr. Hirsch ferreted around inside checking me out, we discussed theater or music or the comparative state of medicine in the United States and France. I would look up periodically and watch his dark eyes and thick brush mustache, rather than looking down where his long fingers were probing and prodding.

I left with the coveted prescription.

JONATHAN CAME TO PARIS AS he had told me he would in Barcelona, stopping off on his way back to Argentina. We met in the bar of the Pont-Royal, a luxurious hotel on the rue de Montalembert. The hotel belonged to the same category as the Castiglione across the river where my parents liked to stay, but with an aesthetic that said more men's club than palace. Nothing ornate, nothing braided, nothing gold. In the early 1950s Simone de Beauvoir had gone there to write sometimes, when the big cafés on Saint-Germain had become too crowded—and she too famous. We sipped whiskey neat in heavy tumblers and sat for a long time in round, dark gray armchairs, deep in smoke, as deep as his emotional dilemmas: Was divorce fair to the children?

Later that afternoon, instead of doing the smart thing—leave the hotel, look at antiques on the rue du Bac, or go down to the Seine—we took the elevator to his hotel room. The charm of our days in Barcelona had started to fade. Jonathan wasn't divorced; he didn't know what he wanted. Did I? I was seduced by the idea of the hotel scene, especially the canonical *cinq à sept,* the stolen hours when French people who are married to others have affairs before returning home to dinner. Doing something for the first time was a temptation I could rarely resist, almost as a matter of principle, especially if it seemed quintessentially French.

In the room we undressed quickly as if we both wanted to get the newness over with. Jonathan's attraction diminished as he removed each expensive item: the subtly striped silk tie, the well-cut, full-bodied shirt, the cleverly pleated gabardine trousers. I watched the progression in the mirror over the sleek, art deco bureau. I winced when I saw his naked belly, wide, swollen, covered, as I had suspected, with dark curly hair. This was familiar territory, like the bellies of my father and the men at the beaches of my childhood. My heart skipped an Oedipal beat. The bear-like chest was a pull, tempting me to lean into his arms. But when I reached out instead to touch and to see, I felt the smallest penis I had ever encountered. Admittedly, I had a very limited sample, but Jonathan's was like a thumb. Jonathan read the question in my hand. "Don't worry, it works," he said, as though we were in high school hygiene class learning what happens when the Penis Becomes Erect. Finally, we just merged quickly, aggressively, to cover our upset. It wasn't remotely like dancing in Barcelona.

Nothing had turned out as I had imagined.

When we said good-bye, Jonathan mentioned casually that his visit to Paris was not only to see me. There was another woman he had become involved with on an earlier trip, and he had to see her to figure out what he wanted. Later I reported to my parents that he was still involved with his wife. "I was, of course, disappointed at the time, but my experience is useful occasionally. If Jonathan couldn't be honest or strong at this stage of the game, he wasn't worth the effort. I'm not interested in this kind of emotional weakness. In fact, it makes me sick." What made me sick was the shock of rejection. I wasn't going to tell them about the real hurt of the Other Woman. The Wife was bad enough.

That winter, Jonathan sent me pictures he had taken of me in Barcelona at Gaudí's Parc Güell, which we had both loved. In his letter he said how much as a photographer he admired the one of me in profile. Despite the flattering camera angle, I could see a deep line forming between my eyebrows. I looked slightly pained, as though I were about to burst into tears. I remembered worrying as I watched him snap pictures of me whether I could desire him the way he said he desired me. I was tired of boy-children and he was a man. After praising his talent as a photographer, Jonathan struck an apologetic note: "I have been thinking of you often and kicking myself for what I did in Paris. But one must take the consequences of one's actions." And then, in the spring, a telegram. He was stopping in Paris on his way to New York to see his children. Would I meet him at Orly between planes? Maybe we could have another chance.

Meeting in an airport appealed to me the way movie scenes always did—I had wept uncontrollably when I said good-bye to Bernard there earlier that summer—but Jonathan had wounded me and I didn't think that it would be the last time. His life was complicated by geography and children. It would be just like the libertines in eighteenth-century novels: they'd hurt you, apologize, and then do it again. I was more enchanted by the concept—older, accomplished, worldly—than by the reality of the man I had gone to bed with at the Pont-Royal. I sent a telegram saying that I would be out of the country.

Etiquette

I BRAGGED ABOUT EXPERIENCE, AND I knew how stories turned out in novels. I was still a slow learner when it came to men.

Philippe had a close friend, Jean, with a hyphenated last name, aristocratic origins, and family property; because of the intimacy between the two men, my parents met Jean almost as soon as they met Philippe, just as I did. Jean and I had been having lunch occasionally, in a casual, friend-of-the-family way. (He was, in fact, another of the friends who had met Bernard, but I had not mentioned this to my parents; their knowing about Philippe and Anne was bad enough.) Jean seemed to know I had slept with Philippe. Even with the intervening years, I was devastated when Jean told me that the night I spent in Philippe's apartment, from the piano playing to breakfast in bed, was part of a routine.

"He always does that when Anne is in the south," he explained. I tried to look cynical, or at least indifferent.

Physically, Jean was the opposite of Philippe—plump and lacka-daisical. Men, I had concluded, came in two modes: fat and thin, bear and stork, manly and boyish. Bears always seemed more comforting, as though they were offering safety and protection, but in the end that didn't make them more reliable. Look what had happened with Jona-than! He had that teddy-bear look, but teddy bears can knock you down with a blow. Unlike Philippe, Jean didn't grope me in the car. In fact, he didn't seem attracted to me at all. It was relaxing to be outside a sexual scenario after my experiments with Jonathan and Philippe.

Jean took me to expensive restaurants near his office (he worked for his father and didn't seem to work very hard) at the Place de la Madeleine, where he instructed me in the finer points of French table manners. You sip wine, not swallow it with big gulps like milk; you don't put your knife down when you eat—you keep fork and knife going at the same time and you place them both neatly on the plate when you are done. You never cut your salad with a knife; you fold the leaves like an envelope. When you put cheese on bread, only small pieces of each, of course, you take a small bite of the bread with the cheese, not a big chunky bite, the way we ate buttered rye bread at home, for instance. These were refinements well beyond not picking up a piece of chicken with my fingers. All in all, meals with Jean took a long time (one lunch lasted from 1 to 5 PM, as I reported to my par-ents), not only because every course had its own difficulties to nego-tiate, but also because wine in the middle of the day was relaxing. Besides, we found each other amusing.

Jean sometimes took the occasion to instruct me in matters of the heart, as if I were still an absolute beginner in these matters of French men and love: the difference between *aimer bien* and *aimer*, those crucial gradations of feelings. When he said, "Je vous aime bien," which he often did, that only meant he was fond of me. But even *very* fond of me was not the same as just plain, unmodified by an adverb, *aimer*. There was the difference between *aimer* and *être amoureux*, love and being in love. And then there was *plaire* (this one was the hardest to get), "to please," as in "You turn me on" (what Philippe had said about his feelings, if you could call that feelings). Jean liked me a lot, he wanted me to understand, but wasn't in love with me, and he was almost engaged to be married.

In late September, after a particularly successful meal—almost no mistakes in food etiquette—Jean took me to the Hermès shop on the Faubourg Saint-Honoré and rewarded me with a big square silk scarf—the classic thirty-six-inch *carré* that Grace Kelly had made famous. Although I wasn't entranced by the Hermès style—saddles, stirrups, nooses—standing with Jean at the counter as he selected the right combination of colors and images without a thought to price, I felt a kind of thrill, as if I had been magically transported into a world I had never imagined. My mother bought designer scarves at a huge discount from one of the perfume places in the ninth arrondissement, geared to American tourists, where you climb one flight up to do business. I had never gone shopping with a man, not to mention an older man, and been given an expensive present. Jean showed me how to tie the scarf, a gift in itself.

I enjoyed being led around and feeling out of my depth. I didn't have to make anything happen.

One afternoon, having polished off a bottle of Bourgeuil, Jean was too tired to go back to the office and asked if he could rest in my room. We walked across the Pont Alexandre III, another relic of Third Republic extravagance, like my beloved Eiffel Tower. As we crossed the bridge I decided I wouldn't sleep with Jean if he wanted to share me with Philippe, after the fact. Was I utterly without will, drifting from one bed to another, hoping that these signs of affection would turn into something more intense? Hadn't the man told me he was almost engaged? So then why did he want to come to my tiny room?

Jean fell asleep on my bed. He left in time for dinner with Marthe, his fiancée-to-be, the youngest daughter of his father's business partner. "But let's keep having lunch," he said, as he rushed out the door, embarrassed at having dozed from five to seven. "You have a lot to learn."

Soon after the siesta in my room, Jean and I had dinner with Philippe and Anne in their apartment. I brought them a hostess gift my parents had asked me to deliver—an ashtray with a goofy ceramic frog wearing glasses and smoking. Their note said that the animal reminded them of Philippe, their favorite "frog" friend. Everyone loved it, I told my parents, especially Philippe.

I was beginning my third year in Paris. The concierge from rue de l'Université had told me about a maid's room coming free just around the corner. My new room was located in an art deco building on avenue Sully Prud'homme, a quiet street near the Quai d'Orsay. Unlike the creaky, claustrophobic affair at rue de l'Université, the building's wood-paneled elevator, set back in the embrace of a wide curving staircase, could hold more than two people, and also took you down. The room was furnished with freshly painted furniture and the sink had hot running water.

I loved my room, but I didn't love my life.

The fellowship interlude was over and I had resumed my old job at Lycée Racine. Going back to the lycée felt like a holding pattern, something to do while taking stock and recovering from the failures of my sentimental education. I was good at school, teaching, and passing exams, but what, really, was I becoming? I couldn't see a bigger picture, a map that led anywhere. Paris offered me the possibility, I had hoped, of being someone *not* my parents' daughter. And yet everything I did to separate from them tied me to them more tightly. Jean's siesta in my room was another example of how not to get what I wanted, if only I knew. Instead, it kept me anchored in their story.

"The Flesh Is Sad, Alas"

RETURNING TO THE LYCÉE MIGHT have represented a step backward in my career narrative, had I been pursuing one. But I settled for liking the girls and the free lunch that was served daily in the teachers' common room. This time I made a friend, Nathalie Lévi. Nathalie was from Morocco. She taught Spanish, and we shared some of the same pupils. An immediate connection sprang up between us, as if we had been related or had known each other from elsewhere. We even looked something alike, people said. We were certainly the only teachers under twenty-five and, as far as we could tell, the only Jews on the faculty.

One Friday afternoon as we were leaving the building together, I suggested we get together over the weekend.

"I never do things on the weekend," Nathalie said. "I have a little girl who is taken care of by a family just outside of Paris." Nathalie lived in a *foyer* for *filles mères* and their infants, but after the age of three the children had to leave.

"You can come with me, if you'd like," Nathalie added. "It's just a short train ride from Saint-Lazare."

I was surprised by the casual tone in which Nathalie described her situation. We were less alike than I had imagined.

"You didn't want to have an abortion?"

"I tried, believe me. I even went to the hospital for an emergency appendectomy. They could have done it then and no one would have known. But the surgeon was Catholic and refused. He told me so after the operation."

"What about the father?"

"He had already left town. He doesn't know he has a daughter, and I doubt that he would care."

I hesitated to ask whether her family knew.

"Look, this child wanted to be born. And when she's older, I'll take her to Morocco to meet my mother. For now, I'm on my own."

I measured the distance between us. We were the same age, but Nathalie was an adult.

"I don't see how you manage on our salary," I said.

"Oh, I do tutoring jobs," she said. "It works out."

I could never finish the month. Even without a child to support like Nathalie, the lycée salary was not enough. Despite my Seberg fixation, I was not about to peddle the *Tribune* on the Champs-Élysées. Determined, after my declarations of independence, not to ask my parents for money, I answered a want ad in the *Tribune* for "dynamic, experienced, and reliable" English teachers. I wound my hair into a librarian's chignon and ironed a white Oxford button-down shirt for the interview.

THE ENGLISH LANGUAGE FOUNDATION, OTHERWISE known as ELF, was a one-man operation. James Donovan had been living in Paris long enough to have figured out that there was a growing market for anglophones who could teach English to French businessmen with jobs in companies where knowledge of English was key to advancement. Unlike the Berlitz schools, which held courses in their own locales, ELF sent out a small army of young native English speakers to the workplaces themselves, to the suburbs of Paris, sometimes as far as Normandy, where several major oil companies with ties to the United States had settled. The office itself had a good address—a quiet street near the Eiffel Tower—but the interview was held in a room whose furniture seemed to have been rented by the hour. The only thing that looked fresh was the letterhead with "ELF" emblazoned across the top of the page in bold capital letters. James Donovan sat behind his desk dressed in a brown herringbone tweed jacket, white button-down Oxford shirt (like mine), and brown gabardine pants, looking the part of an American academic: his calling card. The only thing missing was the pipe.

The next day, I was showered with a flurry of *pneus* at my room and at school from the director, wanting to follow up, he said, on the interview. Most people still lived without telephones. The pneumatic mail system was astonishingly efficient, but also incredibly romantic. Telegrams could be romantic too, of course, but they had been ruined for me by my parents, who fired one off every time they hadn't heard from me in a week: "What's wrong? Send news immediately." Telegrams had started to feel like anonymous death threats, pasted words complete with misspellings as the messages went through from English to French operators. But *pneus*, handwritten notes propelled by compressed air, traveled instantly through tubes to the post office nearest the home of the person you wanted to reach. The mail carrier hand-delivered your personal missive to the door within the day, sometimes within hours. Jim Donovan's *pneus* seemed somewhat excessive in number and tone; they were also strangely persuasive. He was sure I would like the teaching. Couldn't he tell me more about it over a drink?

We met at Ruc, a big café situated on the square opposite the Gare Saint-Lazare, just down the street from Lycée Racine. I had passed by the café, easily recognizable by the black letters that spelled out its name on a bright red awning, many times on my way to the bus stop. It was clever of Jim, I noted, to choose a place near school, removing one of my excuses for saying no. He was grading papers at a table near the window in the corner of the café. I observed him through the glass panes and almost didn't go in. ELF teaching was likely to mean a lot of dark early mornings, which I hated, and I had just successfully eliminated my 8:00 AM classes from my schedule at the lycée. I lingered on the threshold. I needed the money. Teaching businessmen couldn't be worse than tutoring failing lycée pupils, or translating the reports of experiments from a lab in experimental embryology, a well-paying job that my friend Nicole had told me about. At least businessmen were adults—and men. You never knew. Anyway, another interview didn't commit me to anything. I opened the heavy glass door toward me and entered the café.

Donovan was smoking Mecarillos, little Swiss cigars, without inhaling. I sat down and took out a fresh pack of Disque Bleu filtre. I loved the idea of the hard-core Gauloises that Sartre smoked, but the bitter little bits of tobacco and paper sticking to my tongue had finally defeated me.

"I've never seen a woman smoke as much as you do," he said, lighting my cigarette from a large box of wooden matches. "Is that an act?"

"Why would I put on an act?" It annoyed me that he thought I was trying to impress him, but I decided to take the smoking remark as an awkward compliment. Maybe his aggressiveness was more a style he affected out of shyness than an actual assault on my personality.

"Your background impressed me at the interview, but I have one concern," he said, striking a warmer note. "Do you think," he asked, almost paternally, "you might be a little young to deal with men in their late thirties and early forties?"

"I can handle French men," I said, with my best imitation Seberg smile.

Jim was heavy, though not quite so portly as Jonathan. In his case, it was more professorial paunch than Michelin tire. His beard and hair, which had started out red, were flecked with gray, and he looked old, older than he actually was. I was shocked when he said he was only thirty-four. He had grown up in a Boston suburb, the oldest of four brothers and sisters in a working-class Irish family, and had been living in France since the mid-1950s, after a stint in Korea.

Taking each other's measure at the café table, we proceeded to argue about everything, almost coming to blows about which poet wrote the line "La chair est triste, hélas, et j'ai lu tous les livres."

"Baudelaire, of course," I said quickly, thinking back to the seminar I had taken in my first year, and desperately trying to remember what poem the line came from. Who else would have written, "The flesh is sad, alas, and I've read all the books"?

"Mallarmé," Jim said, without hiding the palpable pleasure that being right gave him. "It's true that the themes are Baudelairean," he added faux-ruefully.

I recognized the signs of the Superior Man, the smile that couldn't be completely repressed, and the mocking little tilt of the head that David never resisted either. I asked Jim where he had gone to school. He said he had read all of French poetry by himself, at night, while he was in the army. I supposed that was possible. I'd studied with a professor at Harvard summer school who said he had read all of Proust in the navy. I had planned to leave the interview in time to finish registering for classes at the Sorbonne that afternoon, but I accepted Jim's offer to take me to lunch and then to drive me to the Latin Quarter on his scooter.

All through lunch, I had a case of the severe cramps that had become my frequent companion ever since I had moved to Paris. I had undergone a series of tests, but after many sessions in which chalky liquids were pumped backward into my body with Sadean vigor as I shivered on stainless steel tables, nothing seemed identifiably wrong. Dr. Finkelstein, whom Philippe had recommended, concluded that my *crises* were probably caused by "unconscious tension." I shrugged off his diagnosis—I was living the life I wanted—but I took the prescription for Valium.

"Great literary discussion, a very charming guy," I reported to my parents after meeting Jim.

I was a sucker for men armed with facts, no matter what they looked like. At the same time I also felt diminished by their knowledge. It wasn't enough to know everything though, I'd console myself every time I missed a reference or a date. Didn't you also have to be able to do something with it? David was paralyzed by all the books he had read. It was too early to tell what else was in Jim's library, and what he could do with it.

I took the job.

I fell in love with my first class: five men classified in the French business world as *jeune cadre dynamique*. These success-oriented men in middle management were around Jim's age, married, with kids. Learning to speak English fluently was essential if they were to keep climbing the corporate ladder. Classes were held at company headquarters three days a week before the workday; if dark 8 AM mornings were hard for me, they were harder still for the men, who all lived in the suburbs. But they were motivated, and I was captivated by their motivation. I crossed the flirtatious ingénue persona ironically with that of the strict schoolmarm and it worked. We all sat around a glass-topped table and pretended to make business conversation. I brought long white sheets of paper that I draped over an easel and wrote out my examples with colored markers.

When later that winter Leo returned from his sojourn in New York, I introduced him to Jim. By then Leo and I were more pen pals than ex-lovers (in the end, he was much better as a friend than as a boyfriend), and I hoped he would like Jim. More than just liking, I wanted to know what he thought of Jim. I hadn't made up my mind—there was something strange, hard to place about him—and despite the initial awkwardness of the situation, I brought the three of us together for drinks a few times at Le Dôme, Leo's favorite café, not far from Jim's apartment in Montparnasse. The two men, both determined ex-pats, quickly appreciated each other ("I dig him," Leo actually said), and I took Jim's acquiescence to Leo's place in my life as a sign of approval.

They shared the exile's passion for Paris, a Paris that was never fully Parisian, dotted as it was by American outposts—Le Drugstore on the Champs-Élysées, Haynes's soul food restaurant near the rue des Martyrs, the American library on Place de l'Odéon, the American Hospital, Le centre américain on boulevard Raspail, and above all, American Express, the most reliable place to get mail when you were between addresses, with the warmest bathrooms in Paris (the only public bathroom Leo used, he said). These locations provided a kind of internal set of references, a map within a map that ex-pats had constructed as a safe geography within the city.

Jim asked Leo, who had shown us photographs taken during his Easter odyssey, to come to a few of the classes and shoot pictures of me teaching, pictures Jim could use to create an advertising brochure for the school. In every shot, a pack of cigarettes and a large box of wooden matches sit on the table along with a copy of *Essential English*, a daily calendar, a pencil sharpener, and my Woody Allen–style glasses with black plastic frames. Most of the men smoked as much as I did, and the ashtrays were always overflowing with butts. The French believed that only *les blondes*—cigarettes made from light tobacco (American, English, Dutch)—were bad for you.

The one man in the class who didn't smoke was also my pet. In Leo's photographs he beams at me with the eager intensity of the good student, wanting to know, wanting to please. He was the smartest in the bunch, the best at English, and the natural leader of the little group of men who had been selected for the English classes. The others looked up to him, as if seeking his approval, as if he were their boss. He sported the snappiest ties, the crispest white shirts, and a blazer with slacks instead of slouchy suits shiny from wear. Monsieur Kirili—we were always "Monsieur" and "Mademoiselle"—was the kind of intensely gentle man I never got involved with in my out-of-school life, even though I sometimes could feel the pull. I was disarmed by the man's sweetness. Marry someone nice, my father repeated, whenever I asked who might meet his standards. "Nice" was not in my emotional vocabulary. Teaching, it turned out, was.

Teaching was one of those narrow but secure paths into the future for nice girls, a step up from typing or shorthand. A woman could always fall back on teaching, as my mother put it. You could teach if your husband fell on hard times; you could teach while waiting to get married. There was no teacher—certainly not a French teacher—I remotely wanted to be, and yet teaching had always seemed my fate. When I needed to earn money, teaching was the only thing that came to mind. In my senior year at Barnard, I had succumbed to the logic of the "fall back on" model and had taken courses in the education program. But what I liked about teaching had nothing to do with security. Standing in front of a class of junior high school students for practice teaching at New Lincoln, a progressive private school on the Upper West Side, I was shocked the very first day to experience an almost archaic pleasure. The structure in which *I* was the teacher and *they* were the students felt immediately right—like being the bossy older sibling, but authorized to push the younger kids around.

I still remember from that first class—no doubt because of his famous father, Zero—the responsive face of blond, curly-headed Josh Mostel, as the rhythms of French verb conjugation registered in his brain. Mainly, though, I was pierced by the sensation of standing there and being in charge.

With a different body, I might have become a dominatrix.

November 22, 1963

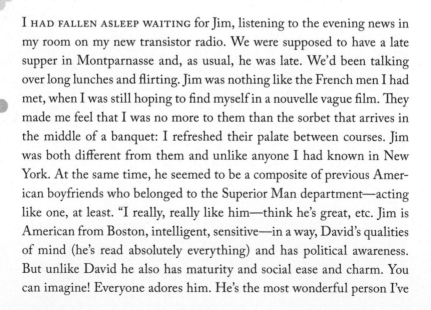

I HAD FALLEN ASLEEP WAITING for Jim, listening to the evening news in my room on my new transistor radio. We were supposed to have a late supper in Montparnasse and, as usual, he was late. We'd been talking over long lunches and flirting. Jim was nothing like the French men I had met, when I was still hoping to find myself in a nouvelle vague film. They made me feel that I was no more to them than the sorbet that arrives in the middle of a banquet: I refreshed their palate between courses. Jim was both different from them and unlike anyone I had known in New York. At the same time, he seemed to be a composite of previous American boyfriends who belonged to the Superior Man department—acting like one, at least. "I really, really like him—think he's great, etc. Jim is American from Boston, intelligent, sensitive—in a way, David's qualities of mind (he's read absolutely everything) and has political awareness. But unlike David he also has maturity and social ease and charm. You can imagine! Everyone adores him. He's the most wonderful person I've known in years." I was flattered by Jim's attention and only occasionally wary. Sometimes he was too charming. Around the edges of my consciousness, I felt a kind of danger—like the constant brush with local traffic when you ride a scooter, a faint breeze of urban anxiety. I couldn't tell whether I was attracted to him or to the idea that he had been sketching out what a great team we'd make. He seemed to be talking about the future of ELF, but sometimes when he held my hand for emphasis, I wasn't sure.

By the time Jim knocked at the door of my room, he had already heard the announcement of Kennedy's assassination. He walked in without saying a word and knelt on the floor next to my bed. He put his head on my lap. I thought he just wanted comfort, to feel close, and I put my hand on his head. Instead, Jim looked up and lifted my skirt, burrowing in between my thighs. I was startled by the sudden move to intimacy. I stood up, smoothing down the pleats of my plaid skirt. His eyes flickered hurt. "Not now," I said, catching his hand. "We have to find a television." We drove to an Irish bar where we could watch the news coverage of the assassination with others.

We spent the night at Jim's place in Montparnasse. I wasn't ready to sleep with Jim, but neither of us wanted to be alone. The assassination pushed us forward. When I watched him sleeping afterward, I couldn't help thinking that he looked vulnerable the way beached whales do when they've lost their way and wash up stranded on the shore. Undressed, Jim's body, I saw, was pear-shaped—the low and wide center of gravity inherited from generations of peasant ancestors that I feared for myself. I preferred him tweeded and professorial, his corpulence disguised by the forgiving lines of a custom-made suit.

Early the next morning, Jim woke me up while it was still dark, holding a cup of tea. He was wearing a raggedy, dark blue terrycloth bathrobe against which the pale skin around his collarbone almost gleamed. I reached out to touch the soft, unprotected spot beneath his Adam's apple, always covered by his shirt and tie, even on Sundays. I wanted to explore this white patch on his body. He took my hand and brought it to his lips. "Ma petite femme," he said gravely. I didn't ask him what he meant.

THE FRENCH HAD BEEN EXCITED by Kennedy and entranced by Jackie, whose French origins seemed to explain her spectacular sense of style. De Gaulle made a joke of referring to the American president as though he were only the man who had accompanied Jackie Kennedy to Paris. The French were mystified by how the protection of a president could be so inefficient. They immediately imagined a conspiracy theory.

I wrote home the following day, proud to share the news from my side of the Atlantic.

> *I hadn't had time to send my letter when the news of Kennedy's assassination came over the radio. I was able to follow the reports from the first "flash" to the confirmation of his death. Today the radio has not ceased to talk, speculate and lament. People were stunned and heartbroken. Everyone seemed to have admired and more, liked Kennedy, finding him "jeune et sympathique." Even the vegetable sellers are upset and talking about it.*

At the lycée, pupils and teachers came up to me in the hall and expressed their sympathy, shaking their heads in disbelief and pressing my hand as though I had personally suffered a tragic loss. Until then, Irish American associations had had almost no content for me. There was only Marilyn Wisely, a girl I had liked in junior high school, whose nose, to my amazement, pointed straight up into the air. I realized that through Jim, the Kennedy story had become unexpectedly close.

The fact that we had experienced the assassination together in Paris gave our couple narrative a ready-made history that had nothing to do with sex.

Steak Tartare

I THOUGHT I HAD LEARNED all there was to know about eating in restaurants from Jean, but Jim brought a foreigner's intensity to the table. He had grown up eating boiled meat and overcooked vegetables; meals were to be endured, not savored. His Irish mother seemed to have perfected the same cooking skills as my father's Jewish one, whose broiled liver, according to my mother, had the consistency of shoe leather. In photographs, the two women resembled each other: bitter widows with sullen faces whose older sons had fled their presence.

Unlike my father, who always defended his mother's culinary efforts, Jim had no nostalgia for home cooking. The first of Jim's restaurant-eating principles in fact required that you order only something you couldn't possibly make yourself. You might crave something absolutely simple—a piece of grilled fish and boiled potatoes, for instance—but you had to choose the complication: sole wrapped in sorrel, swimming in cream. Otherwise, what was the point of going to the restaurant? Jim would ask rhetorically. He wanted to feel the effort that had gone into making a dish. Sometimes, on the same principle—ordering what you would never make for yourself—we would work our way through a huge *choucroute alsacienne*. In the beginning, I guiltily went along with this dish—a favorite of Jim's—to prove to myself that I had transcended the dietary rules that had regulated my childhood. But I was not happy consuming an entire inventory of pork products; I could almost see the diagram of a whole pig floating above the steaming platter of sauerkraut.

Jim demonstrated a certain eccentricity in relation to the order of a French menu. Violating protocol, he would scorn the appetizers, for instance, and replace them with a vegetable, say, *haricots verts*, meant to be a side dish. The waiters looked down their noses at us—one doesn't eat string beans before the main course—but in the end they capitulated to Jim's manner. Whatever strangeness manifested itself in the sequence of dishes was compensated for by his knowledge of the *plateau de fromage* and his authority about the wine list. He always chose a runny cheese, usually dirty-sock smelly like Époisses; a tiny goat cheese, chalky without being dry (my favorite); and a firm cheese like Morbier, with its distinctive stripe of ash down the middle, to provide a mild hiatus between sharper tastes. (The waiter commiserated with Jim over the fact that one really couldn't have a separate wine for each cheese.) At first I cringed when Jim lingered over the cheese, but cheese talk is a language and Jim loved talking it. He was the chooser; I was the taster. If we were to continue as a couple, I had to be educated. With Jean, the point of my table instruction was manners; he cared less about what I ate than how. With Jim, the target was my palate.

I let Jim persuade me to take over an evening class that one of his teachers had to give up for family reasons. The teacher was getting married and his wife expected him home for dinner. My reward for teaching at night after a long day at the lycée was that Jim would pick me up at the end of class on his scooter and take me to dinner at La Coupole, around the corner from his apartment. Steak tartare was one of the restaurant's signature dishes, and it became our ritual for late supper after the class. The formally dressed waiter would position himself by the table, and from a special stand mix chopped onion, capers, Worcestershire sauce, and a raw egg into the raw, chopped meat on his silver tray. Steak tartare represented the worst possible combination of ingredients for my delicate digestive system, but I had decided that what mattered was not *what* I ate but the mood in which I was eating. This wasn't exactly scientific, nor what Dr. Finkelstein had recommended, but it felt true. In fact, the mood theory, as I saw it, was somewhat more complicated. If it was all a question of mood, I reasoned, it was not so much the mood I was in while eating as it was the previous mood. Sometimes the *crise* would come on in response to what had happened earlier that day. I might feel relaxed contemplating the steak tartare, but if my stomach had been in knots two hours before while I was teaching, I would soon be feeling the effects of my anxiety. Pay later, the famous rule of consequences. I could fool my brain but not my gut. Invariably, halfway through dinner I would wend my way to the romantic art deco *toilettes* and behind the dark doors quickly insert two suppositories of muscle relaxants, the embarrassing French solution to pain. The little waxy yellow bullets, as I thought of them, shot their relief with astonishing speed.

In the Coupole's cavernous space, where smoke and loud conversation made me feel at the center of something ineffably fashionable, I would always take my place on the banquette, leaning into the padded leather backrest at an angle sufficient to release the pressure around my waist. Naturally, it never occurred to me that eating with Jim was making me anxious. I wanted badly to prove to him that I was (or could become) his equal at the table, that I could keep up with eating and drinking, that I could eat what repulsed Americans—raw meat, brains, sweetbreads, kidneys. (I actually got to like kidneys, even though in the beginning I ate them just to show off.) I wanted Jim to see me as an equal, despite the fact that in his eyes I was a novice eater as well as a novice teacher.

Eating what was bad for me was my way of showing love. I hoped that I was eating my way into his heart.

Jim periodically observed my classes, as he did with the other teachers, and often at dinner, he would grade my performance according to the pedagogic principles he had elaborated for the school. It was a relief and a torment to review the lessons and draw the moral. I wanted to be a better teacher, but I hated being corrected. The contradiction pulled me in and pushed me out.

Three glasses of Burgundy and the required cheese course later, the waiter would serve my weekly reward, one of two elaborate desserts: Baked Alaska (that the French name moved to Scandinavia, *l'omelette norvégienne*), which had to be ordered at the beginning of the meal, or, if I hadn't felt up to deciding, *le hot fudge*—vanilla ice cream with hot chocolate sauce and shaved, toasted almonds. Both combined warm and cold sensations of sweetness, which made me shiver with delight and dissolved the lingering tensions of the workday.

My pleasure in these treats, which were designed for adults but satisfied childhood tastes, was old as well as new. My mother made a dessert she called a bombe. The recipe, which came from an old New York Italian restaurant, involved scooping out an orange, cutting up the fruit, and returning it to the hollowed orange with ice cream. Then a meringue would sit on top of the orange, which was set in a pan surrounded by ice cubes and heated in the oven. The warm meringue melted the ice cream as the ice cream cooled the fruit, suavity itself. The bombe was the crowning touch of my mother's many dinner parties, grand affairs for large groups of friends that lasted late into the night. My sister and I loved the bombe, but that didn't prevent us from complaining—"that again?"—when the orange appeared twice in one month. There was something about being with Jim, who was in manner so quintessentially adult, that triggered the memory of childhood tastes in me.

At the end of the Coupole dinners, Jim would have a shot of Armagnac; he preferred to drink his calories. Logy with food and wine, we would weave the few blocks home on the Lambretta. I rested my cheek on the rough tweed surface of Jim's wide back, feeling safe, even though he was usually quite drunk.

"Marry Someone Interesting"

"MARRY SOMEONE INTERESTING," MY MOTHER used to say (resigned to the fact that a doctor or lawyer would never appeal), but someone interesting who was also independently wealthy. That was the path to becoming a woman of leisure thanks to one's husband's income (her dream). When pressed, my mother never came up with a good example of such a person. Jim at least was interesting, and disarming.

For one thing, he loved to alternate between the high- and low-culture pleasures of Paris. One day I'd receive a *pneu* from Jim telling me to join him at the still-newish Drugstore on the Champs-Élysées for a hamburger, followed by the latest James Bond movie, another that he had managed to get tickets for Beckett's *Happy Days* at the Odéon with Madeleine Renaud. I cherished the tiny folded missives covered with Jim's equally tiny, crabbed script. I was allowed to refuse the summons that sometimes felt like a subpoena—but I rarely said no.

I liked the extremes of his tastes, even when they made me unhappy.

On special occasions, Jim took me out for a very expensive meal that would be billed to the business. I would be given a menu with no prices—as though I were a mistress or even a wife. Jim would never tell me the price of the dishes; those appeared only on his menu, since he was the bill payer. He wanted me to choose purely on the grounds of desire. The first time this happened, we had gone to Chez Garin, a small two-star restaurant not far from Notre-Dame, to celebrate a contract with a new company. The selection was limited, but I found it almost impossible to decide what to eat without seeing the prices. I had been trained in childhood never to order the most expensive thing on the menu, which meant I never really knew what I wanted. I closed the large cloth menu. Since Jim was convinced I didn't understand anything about French food anyway, he was happy to order for me. Besides, I knew he wanted me to model my desires on what he wanted my desires to be. Maybe that was my desire, too, or part of it. How could you know what you liked or didn't like if you didn't know what you were supposed to like?

"Madame," Jim began, looking at the waiter and referring to me in the third person. We weren't married, but I was promoted to the category as a sign meant to inspire respect.

"Madame," Jim informed the unsmiling waiter, "will begin with the *terrine de canard*." I didn't really care for terrine—like pâté, terrine reminded me of chopped liver—but it was a house specialty listed as such in the *Guide Michelin*.

"For the main course, a *truite soufflée*." Jim knew I prefer grilled fish but again, it was highlighted in the *Guide*, our secular bible. Besides, you could have grilled fish at any brasserie, or even at home. Jim might be a food iconoclast, but he worshiped the guides for restaurants with stars and memorized their special features before arriving at the restaurant. At Garin, where you could feel the chef's domination in every detail, Jim seemed intimidated. He docilely ordered the *côte de boeuf vigneronne* (also in the guide) at the waiter's suggestion (via the chef, of course), even though he had told me he didn't want to have beef. The waiter nodded approval; he didn't need to write down the order.

We were the only Americans that night, and I could hear our conversation above the murmur of the French diners.

Why did expensive restaurant versions of food matter so much to Jim? It was as though every mouthful of haute cuisine took him further from the good Catholic little boy he thought for so long he was doomed to be. Every elegantly wrought morsel was proof that he had escaped his mother's kitchen. Still, the escape had been a narrow one, I thought, embracing him from behind as I hung on at the back of the scooter in the dark winter night.

We didn't always eat at fancy places. Sometimes we'd go to a student-run Vietnamese restaurant in the rue des Carmes, behind the Pantheon. The food collective was one of the cheapest places to eat in Paris, and a lot less depressing than the government-owned Resto-U, which we still went to with our student cards at the end of the month when we were broke. (With his habitual resourcefulness Jim had managed to finagle a student card, even though his student days belonged to a distant past.) At the collective you ordered from a window when you came in and then moved on to a long communal table. A waiter would bring your dish to the head of the table and call out your name. We cringed when the foreign sound of our American names rang out above the clatter of plates. But Jim's friend, Danh, a Vietnamese philosopher living in Paris, reassured us that the Vietnamese distinguished between the evil American government and the peace-loving American people. Jim took the French view, which had converted its own history in Indochina to wisdom, and I took his, especially when I wrote to enlighten my parents, borrowing his rhetorical flourish: "From here the situation in Vietnam seems absolutely insane—there's a feeling of wonder that American policy can be so blind to reality. All the American columnists with any brains at all have realized that the Vietnamese are only interested in peace, that democracy and communism are unimportant issues by comparison, and that the psychological make-up of the Vietnamese is completely different from ours."

During the Korean occupation, Jim had worked in the army kitchen. He hated the military, but he came out of the war adept with chopsticks.

Jim and I fascinated each other, almost as categories. He was a philo-Semite; I was a nice, middle-class, Jewish girl from the Upper West Side of New York, whose immigrant origins had been transformed by a generation of professionalism and education. Jim's parents had not been educated. His father, who had immigrated to Boston from Ireland as a teenager, died when Jim was eleven. We shared a resistance to the stories our parents had made for us. We couldn't bear to be the people our families wanted us to become.

Europe offered us an escape from our family plots. Jim should have grown up to work for the post office like his father, or, since he was smart, become a priest. I was destined to teach high school French in Manhattan, a small notch above teaching elementary school as my mother did for years when money was tight. Jim had already married and divorced a girl from his neighborhood; I vowed I would never marry anyone from my shtetl.

In what we didn't want, we were a match.

With each other, we left America behind. By early December the attachment precipitated by Kennedy's death had become a relationship I wasn't sure I could define but I knew would displease my parents. As usual, my anticipation of their resistance made me defiant, ready for battle. In the past, they had found ways to make me give up on things (going away to school) and people I thought I loved (David); and, often every cleverly, as they had with Bernard, they had punctured my plans with what sounded like a simple question. I was determined not to let that happen again. It wasn't hard to guess what my parents were going to say about Jim (He's not Jewish; He's too old, What does he do for a living?), but I also knew I had to defend myself in person if I didn't want to continue writing a serial novel by letter.

I had vaunted Jim's qualities, declared how happy I was, painted a glamorous picture of our life together in Paris that convinced even me. It wasn't that I didn't have doubts about Jim. Sometimes he was too persuasive, too intent on his way of doing things. Yes, I was happy, but I was also anxious, and I couldn't quite say why. But if I was captivated by a story that often felt beyond my control, I wasn't going to let my parents interrupt the narrative just as it was getting started. At the very least, I wanted to see where it would go. Time, I figured, was on my side. I was only twenty-two.

That Christmas, I flew to New York by charter. It took twelve hours and cost $250. I hadn't been home in over two years.

325 Riverside Drive

"WHAT DOES THIS GUY DO, exactly?" my father asked in a predictably skeptical tone, as the four of us sat down to dinner in the kitchen the first night of my return. My younger sister Andrea was still living at home, but she had warned me that I couldn't count on her in a showdown. She was secretly dating a Negro, as we said then, and biding her time until graduation from Barnard, when she planned to move to the East Village and live with him.

"I told you in my letter. He runs a language school."

"Like Berlitz?"

"On a much smaller scale."

My father cleared his throat and wiped his mouth with a napkin.

"What kind of an income does the school generate at this point?" my father asked, reaching for a yellow-lined legal pad, ready to calculate our economic future.

I had no idea.

"My parents were not overly enthusiastic," I wrote in my first letter to Jim, "but I haven't given up."

Jim's letters arrived almost daily. Chagall's painting *Les Fiancés de la Tour Eiffel* had just been issued as a postage stamp. Chagall had left Russia for Paris. His immigrant past gave him the material; the freedom of Paris, the chance to paint the way he wanted to. In Chagall's topsy-turvy universe Paris and the shtetl coexisted within a single vision. The couple lifts off in a tilted pas de deux across a sky populated by fiddlers and horses. A chuppa figured in miniature moves backward into the time of memory under the protective arch of the Eiffel Tower, which seems to disappear upward beyond an invisible horizon.

Every envelope from Jim had the Chagall stamp on it. Jim was always kind of a literalist, in this case taking Marshall McLuhan, who was all the rage, to the letter: the medium is the message. Jim was putting the idea of our marriage on the map by stamp, as it were, without ever asking, bypassing language completely. He wanted my parents to perceive the seriousness of his intentions. My mother would drop the letters on my bed without comment. If she got the message, she wasn't saying.

"My dear little wife," Jim wrote in his first letter, "do you know what you are letting yourself in for?" Jim imagined us as selves without borders, bound without boundaries. I was his exclusive possession, not to be shared with the world. Fusion and exclusion. A *folie à deux,* as the French like to put it. I had never heard this language before from him, or from anyone else, for that matter, though in some ways Jim's desire to blot out the rest of the world reminded me of David's burlap-bag fantasy, his idea for what I'd wear, ideally, if I were not looking to please others— the couple unto itself.

"I Want to Hold Your Hand," the Beatles sang sweetly as our couple story began to unfold.

"From now on, I'm taking you in hand," Sartre said to Simone de Beauvoir in the early days of their relationship. I was waiting for someone to do that for me. Take me in hand and project me with him into a future. True, the two of them never married or actually lived together, but their lives were inextricably linked—that was the main thing.

Here was a man with an idea of how to be two, how two could be one. Jim's fantasy was the motor I needed to become independent of my parents. With Jim on my side, I would have a powerful counterweight to my parents' couple. With Jim, I could stay not only away from them, but away from an America that I now saw through foreign eyes.

Maybe I didn't know what I was getting myself into, as Jim put it, but that was precisely the appeal. Jim's fantasy had a kind of narrative thrust and that was what I needed. I'd worry about the content of the story later.

"He's Not Peter Gay"

Soon after my twenty-third birthday, my parents resumed their campaign for my permanent return to the United States. We had arrived at almost exactly the same point we had one year earlier when I was lobbying for Bernard. In the short term, they wanted me to visit with them over the summer at the Cape; I had refused. My father suggested that we discuss the situation over the phone. Jim drove me to the Hôtel des Postes near the Louvre, the main post office where there wasn't a long wait to make a transatlantic call. He positioned himself near the booth, ready to cheer me on.

The receiver felt heavy in my hand.

"How can you say you are independent," my father began with no preamble, "when you can't even imagine being separated for the space of a summer? I thought you wanted to be independent." We were back to the old struggle.

"You seem to think 'independent' means my doing what you think is right." I positioned the receiver between my ear and neck and waited for his comeback. We were having what the French call *un dialogue de sourds*. We were deaf to each other. But that didn't stop anyone from talking.

"I'm not telling you what to do, I'm just making a suggestion. There's a difference."

"So what's your suggestion?"

"Come back and spend the summer here."

"Listen," I said, gazing desperately at Jim, whom I could see leaning against one of the empty phone booths, reading *Le Monde*. It was like one of those Ionesco plays where people keep repeating the same sentences without noticing. "I already told you, I'm not in the mood for an eight-week separation."

"Then how can you say you're independent?"

"I earn my own living," I said, hoping my father wouldn't remember that they had bailed me out of the previous summer's misery by taking me on vacation.

"Being 'independent,'" I said, "doesn't mean not caring about the person you love." It was hard not to mimic my father's sententiousness. "Jim counts in the equation."

"Of course, he counts," my father said in the deceptively reasonable tone he adopted whenever he totally disagreed with me, "but so do you. You need some perspective."

I didn't want perspective. This was exactly how they had always undermined my decisions. Are you sure? Are you sure? Of course, I wasn't sure. Jim had asked me the right question. I didn't know what I was getting myself into, but wasn't that the point? Wasn't that the definition of freedom? At the very least, I was in love with the idea of me in love with someone who was in love with me and had made his life in Paris. I didn't know more than that, but I didn't want to know.

I had decided to stay on in France if I found another job. I wasn't making enough money to support myself with ELF. Jim's school was still more of a good idea than a source of financial security. Besides, teaching English to businessmen, or the lycée girls, for that matter, had already lost most of its charm. I was halfway through a second graduate degree, the equivalent of a master's in English that I had begun in Poitiers, when for the first time foreigners with advanced degrees were allowed to work in the French university system. Dominique Reza, a professor I had known since Middlebury summer school, encouraged me to apply for a position at the Sorbonne.

That May I was named to the Sorbonne as a *lectrice d'américain* for one year, renewable to two. I took the appointment as a sign that I was meant to stay. Now that I had a job with a regular salary paid by the French government, it felt safe enough to return to America for a few weeks during the summer. Not alone, but with Jim. We would briefly join the parents in Provincetown. Maybe meeting face-to-face would change the tone of the conversation. If I had never known anyone like Jim, neither had they.

WE ALL WENT OUT TO dinner at one of the big noisy lobster places for tourists on the pier that served the ultimate in high kitsch nonkosher food (my mother had long abandoned keeping a kosher kitchen to please her parents). The tables were covered with red-and-white-check tablecloths, and straw-wrapped Chianti bottles hung from the beams in the ceiling. The waitress fitted out each of us with a plastic bib.

My father moved right in with his questionnaire about Mixed Marriages.

"Nancy tells us you have a cousin who's a nun in Ireland," he said, cracking open a lobster claw. "Is religion important to you?"

I realized my father was jumping ahead to the foreskin of future offspring. Jim did too. I could tell by the way he had flushed above his beard, his cheeks pink with embarrassment. We had rehearsed this.

"Actually," Jim said, "my real allegiance is to Reason."

My father looked blank. "Reason?"

"Yes, like the *philosophes*," Jim said.

My father knew about the Enlightenment, but Jim had left him nowhere to go.

I wanted to explain that Jim was enamored of all things Jewish, wished he had been born Jewish, but I knew the conversation was doomed. And how could I say I loved the fact that Jim wasn't remotely Jewish, whatever his crossover fantasies and his laments over his uncircumcised state (*sans coupure*, as he referred to it)?

"How about dessert?" my father finally said, in temporary retreat.

After dinner, I walked Jim back to his room.

"So what do you think?" I asked as we strolled along Commercial Street, the long narrow street leading to the Provincetown Inn, at the east end of town.

"They don't think I'm good enough."

When I got back to the cottage they had rented not far from the inn, my parents were still awake, watching television in the bedroom.

"So what do you think?" I asked, sitting down on the sofa bed they had made up for me in the living room.

"The beard," my mother said, "makes him look as if he's hiding something." My mother could never resist a negative comment on people's appearance.

"But he's interesting, right? You weren't bored at dinner."

"He's too old for you."

"That wasn't the question."

"That stuff about the Enlightenment. It sounds like Peter Gay."

When I was at Barnard, I babysat for Ruth and Peter Gay, who lived near us on the Upper West Side. My mother had long conversations with Ruth on the corner of West End Avenue and 103rd Street.

"But he's not Peter Gay."

"Don't get married," my father said unhappily after a while. "Just live together, if you have to."

Playing House

I DECIDED TO TAKE MY father's grudging "live together" *à la lettre*, even though I knew he did not approve of what he called "shacking up." Jim wanted me to move in with him ("Wouldn't it be more convenient? Closer to the Sorbonne"), and after a few weeks of hesitating (it wasn't that much closer), I agreed. Monique was living with Alain. Wasn't this the next step? True, living with Bernard (and briefly with Leo) hadn't worked out, but did that mean forming a couple with Jim was doomed? How else would I find out? Still, I did not give up my lovely new maid's room and, as with Bernard, kept the address for writing letters home.

Almost exactly a year after the Kennedy assassination, I packed a suitcase of books and clothing and moved into Jim's *deux pièces,* a tiny two-room apartment without a bath, in a tenement building near the Montparnasse train station that was about to be torn down. A faded sign on the building's facade advertised *gaz à l'étage* as an inviting modern feature. Gas meant that the tiny kitchen was supplied with a hot-water heater over the sink and a stove with two burners, but no oven. We had no refrigerator either and, like my neighbors, I shopped daily, hanging perishables outside the window in a *filet*.

The building's toilets were Turkish and located on the landing, halfway between each floor. A permanently open window high on the wall of the air shaft made sweaters a necessity in all seasons. The toilet paper consisted primarily of slick brown sheets, sometimes replaced with torn squares of newspaper, which were less sanitary but more effective. The moment I heard footsteps on the stairs while I was carefully poised squatting over the hole, I instantly pulled the chain and scooted out, trying not to get my feet wet. After a while, I perfected my timing.

In *Breathless*, Belmondo's thuggish but charming character Michel pays Jean Seberg's Patricia the sublimely new wave courtesy of asking for permission to piss in her bathroom sink. That was the option favored by Jim, not that he asked.

Once a week we went to the Bains d'Odessa down the street, where the rooms of sparkling blue-and-white tile radiated cleanliness. Bath attendants in white coats hosed down the tub and the tile floors between clients. Only the attendant was authorized to open the door from the outside. While I loved the strangely peaceful sensation of sinking into the huge tub filled with steaming water, naked in a space I did not control, I never completely relaxed. On the coldest days, I consoled myself with the notion that by going to the public baths, I was shedding a layer of bourgeois propriety along with my week of Parisian grime.

FROM THE BEGINNING, OUR LIFE together was a lot like school. Teacher and pupil, homework and lessons. Elizabeth David's *French Country Cooking* for food, Georges Bataille's *L'Érotisme* for sex.

One of Jim's many food rules was that a meal at home should start with a vegetable. For guests, the preparation of the vegetable demanded an obvious degree of complexity. Glazed turnips satisfied Jim's demands: they were cheap, but prepared à la Elizabeth David, they offered an elegant surprise. David's English hymn to the ingredients of the French countryside combined a commitment to peasant, rather than haute, cuisine with a certain degree of effort required in following the recipes. Good food, she explained in her introduction, is "always a trouble and its preparation should be regarded as a labour of love." David was the perfect mediator during my apprenticeship in the kitchen. Neither complicatedly French nor blandly American, she made me feel I might one day cook like a European.

The recipe for *navets glacés* seemed simple enough. Boil the turnips (the little purple and white ones) and when they are almost ready, put them in a buttered skillet with some of the water they have cooked in, add more butter, and sprinkle them with sugar (using large amounts of butter was one of Elizabeth David's primary cooking strategies). When you cook the turnips at the right temperature (low but not too low) with the right amount of liquid (a little, but not too little), the sauce caramelizes. The tension between the slightly bitter taste of the turnips and the sugar glaze produces an interesting ambiguity, Jim liked to say.

Navets glacés were one of Jim's favorite appetizers. I had made the dish many times and mastered the process, I thought. One fall evening, I set out to glaze the turnips for Jim's oldest French friend, Paul, an unmarried schoolteacher, who was also a member of the Communist Party. Jim had never joined the party, but he always bought their newspaper *L'Humanité* as a gesture of solidarity. The conversation between the two men could have come straight from the pages of Doris Lessing's *The Golden Notebook*. Like the Marxist characters in the novel, Jim and Paul took themselves for men who bore the weight of the world on their shoulders, figuring out how it should be run. They respected women, of course—that was the party line—but somehow women missed most of the conversation by being in the kitchen.

That night, while the men were having drinks and olives in the living room, I bent over the stove watching desperately for a positive sign. No matter what I did, the turnips just lay there, staring back at me, stubbornly pale and resistant. They refused to glaze; it was war, and I was losing. I could smell the anxiety rising from my armpits. Why was this happening now in front of company? Finally, as I was about to

leave the stove and confess my failure, the glaze took. I quickly sprin-
kled parsley over the turnips and raced around the corner into the living room to serve them. In the flush of culinary triumph, I skidded on
the shiny black linoleum floor (previously washed and waxed by me).
The earthenware dish in which I had arranged the turnips to complete
the peasant effect slipped from my hands and the turnips scattered in
all directions. One rolled under the couch. I looked at Paul, hoping for
sympathy, while Jim charged furiously into the kitchen himself to impro-
vise Elizabeth David's *tomates provençales en salade*—"poor substitute,"
he muttered apologetically to our guest. But Paul rose from the couch,
swiftly scooped the turnips off the floor and, sitting down at the table,
declared them "délicieux."

This gallant gesture completely changed my mind about Communists.

On the Road

JIM WORE ONLY BLACK SHOES and black socks. Soon after I started spending time in the apartment, I voluntarily preempted the task of washing his socks. I would pile up a load of black socks in the pasta pot to soak and simmer them over a low flame. When I had wrung the socks out in the sink and dried them on the line strung outside the kitchen window, the real work began: making pairs out of almost, but perversely never completely, identical socks. I studied the long black socks as carefully as a text, looking for the pattern, the clocks or arrows that would distinguish one pair from the other.

I think I knew the socks were not a text.

Sundays Jim cruised the flea markets at the gates of Paris for his personal collections: Majolica plates, wooden shoe molds, *porte-couteaux* in the form of animals. Being with Jim was entering a world already designed, complete with *objets*.

All I had to do was fit myself into it.

Outside the apartment, free from the domestic script both of us had fallen into, Jim was the companion I had fantasized about. We pursued his tastes and followed his enormous appetite. We drove to Deauville to hear Jacques Brel sing "Ne Me Quitte Pas." We sat close enough to see him sweat. In Brel's honor we traveled to Belgium to eat mussels and *frites*.

More often, we traveled south by scooter. I'd be squeezed in between Jim's large back and the camping gear, my nose burning in the sunlit air. The scooter lacked the thrill of Leo's motorcycle, but maybe that was the right metaphor for a relationship with a future: the scooter was slower, but steadier. We'd stop at *un camping*, pitch a tent, stand in line to shower, and then ride into town on the scooter as though we just happened to be in the area. I always packed an Orlon dress that rolled into a ball. Jim would put on a fresh white shirt and a tie, and the hours of noise and fatigue on the scooter fell away. After dinner, he would theatrically puff on a Cuban cigar as we walked through the streets.

On one of our trips, we spent the night in Marseille, at La Cité Radieuse, an apartment building designed by Le Corbusier in the 1950s and made out of reinforced concrete. Jim had discovered that a few studios were available for tourists. French friends were always amazed at Jim's insider information. I loved that he knew so much, almost as much as he did.

In the photographs from that stay, Jim's brow is heavily furrowed; the ridges look like tracks made by heavy tires in the sand. He is wearing his terry cloth bathrobe, drinking coffee outside on our balcony from which we could gaze at city views with the Rhône in the background. In the picture he took of me, I'm drinking from a deep white cup and gazing off into the distance. His tie is hanging from the doorknob. Next to the breakfast tray is a half-empty flask of the Irish whisky that always traveled with us. Jim liked to pour himself a nightcap before he went to bed. Sometimes he drank again in the middle of the night if he couldn't fall back to sleep.

We never talked much in the mornings. Jim tried to help me enter the daylight world by bringing me tea while I was still in bed. By that time, he would have been up for hours.

Those were our best times, before the day's activities set our anxieties in motion.

The Letter

JIM HAD OFTEN SAID HE loved and admired me, but whenever the topic of the future came up, marriage was always shrugged off into a vague inevitability. Of course we were going to get married. I wasn't to take the vagueness as a lack of feeling. Jim wanted to be able to provide for me, he said, and things with the school simply weren't at that point. In the meantime, his favorite term of endearment was "my little wife." We even bought an antique gold ring with a tiny amethyst, my birthstone, in Portobello Road on one of our trips to London. I used to spin the ring on my finger, making it look like a wedding band. I didn't care about being married, I said. I could earn my own living.

One day, emptying Jim's pockets to take his jacket to the cleaners, I found a letter from the woman I thought was his ex-wife, writing to Jim as if they were still married, as though he might return to the States to be with her in the near future. I thought this woman was completely in the past tense, but there she was, fully in the present. I sat in the apartment all day waiting for Jim to come home, rigid with rage at the betrayal.

"What does this mean? When we met at Ruc after the interview, you *told* me you were divorced."

"I said we were divor*cing*," he answered evenly, looking at me as if I were slightly retarded, and reaching for the bottle of Jameson sitting on the cupboard in the corner of the living room.

"That's not true. I remember that conversation very well. Do you think I would have moved in with you if I had known you were still married?" Having an affair with a married man was one thing. An affair had its rules, its excitement, and its cachet. But a man who was married without being married was another. He was availably unavailable in what was supposed to be a relationship, not an affair.

"Why are you arguing with me? I said I want to marry you."

"What can that possibly mean if you are married to someone else?"

"I'm not *really* married to someone else."

"That's not what the letter says. It's not what *she* thinks," I objected, pointing to her words on the page. "She wants to buy you a bathrobe!"

"It doesn't matter what she thinks. What matters are my intentions," he said with that air of total conviction that makes you believe it's safe to walk on the newly frozen ice, and pouring himself another glass of whisky.

"But what did you say to her to make her think you were going back to her?"

"I didn't want her to feel bad, and I didn't want her to make problems for the divorce, so I let her think we might get back together once the separation was official."

"That doesn't make any sense."

"Look, the point is, she's not coming back here. She's living with a Negro plumber," Jim added, as though that solved the problem.

"But when are you going to tell her?" I kept on, unconvinced of the plumber's existence. Like the husband in *Gaslight,* who drives his wife insane by making her doubt the evidence of her senses, Jim had the knack of making me feel that I lacked the capacity to distinguish fantasy from reality, despite the words in the letter.

Jim finished his whisky and walked out, letting the heavy door slam behind him. I could hear the concierge muttering in the courtyard, where all sounds were magnified, about the bad manners of "les américains." I thought about going back to my room, but I was hoping Jim would return. I finally fell asleep on the bed with my clothes on. When I woke up at midnight in the empty apartment, I scrawled my rage in lipstick on the bedroom mirror like Elizabeth Taylor in *Butterfield 8:* "Live alone, sleep alone, fuck alone," I ranted in dramatic script. Then I washed my face and took a taxi to my room.

That wasn't the first time Jim had just vanished without an explanation. From the beginning, he would disappear for short periods of time, often on Sunday afternoons. He didn't seem to know—or wouldn't tell me—where he had been or what he had been doing. The disappearing act was worrisome, but my desire to make the story turn out well made me repress what I couldn't incorporate into the weave. The surface reality of the narrative I was spinning about our life as a couple—seeing friends, eating in great restaurants, going to the theater, traveling—was sweeping me along. The story had gathered momentum. What would happen if I stopped now?

Early the next morning, Jim knocked at the door of my room. He was standing in the hallway, looking sheepish, with a huge bunch of red roses. He would make the divorce process official that summer, he said, only a few months away. When I didn't answer, Jim knelt on the floor and laid his heavy head on my knees. I smoothed his forehead, wishing my fingers could decipher the secrets stored there, and at the same time feeling afraid to discover what else the lines might be hiding.

A Million Magic Fingers

WE DECIDED TO MARRY IN Switzerland. Jim explained that the requirements of French bureaucracy would bring unwarranted attention to his previous marriage, and that would only delay things—not that there was any pressing reason not to wait until the summer, when in theory the waiting period for the decree in Boston would be over officially. But after the drama with the letter, Jim wanted to prove his good faith, and I wanted to believe him. In Geneva, the only requirement for a civil marriage was a passport: no blood, no documents. Your word stood in for your history. I took Jim at his.

We informed my parents of our Swiss wedding plans by mail as we left Paris, too late for them to respond or intervene. I knew it was cowardly of me to elope. I also knew that if I gave my parents advance notice, they would want to talk me out of it, urge me to come home, or at least wait for them to arrive. I still remembered the effect of my mother's question about Bernard: "Are you sure you want to marry this boy?" I had been trying to forestall that question by going on the offensive. "I know how you feel, but I must let my feelings dominate. I'm old enough to act according to my own instincts—and if I am wrong, to take the responsibility, consequences of misguided judgment. Please don't start making dire predictions and wringing your hands." This time, I didn't want to be talked out of my desires. "I'm really in love!"

Our combined teaching schedules that spring meant we had time for only one night in Geneva—the night before the wedding. Jim reserved a room at the Victoria, one of the fancy large hotels overlooking Lake Geneva. When we checked into the room, he put the Veuve Cliquot we brought from Paris in the bidet and ran the cold water to keep it cool. After making a toast, Jim lay down on the bed. I lay down beside him. We were both exhausted from the long drive. The beds were fitted out with a device called "A Million Magic Fingers," designed, we thought mockingly, for weary businessmen. Press the button, the directions over the headboard explained, and the mattress would vibrate for five minutes. Why not? Jim pressed the button and, lulled by the activity of the million magic fingers, immediately fell into a deep sleep.

Once launched into operation, the machine would not shut off, no matter what I tried. I was too humiliated to call housekeeping for help. What if they saw the champagne bottle in the bidet? As I listened to Jim snoring, I rehearsed the magic fingers story for my parents—they would recognize themselves in us, in saving the cost of the champagne and the ice bucket—but why did I want to tell my parents about my wedding night? Not that it was my wedding night, since we were doing it all backward, as they would not have hesitated to point out. I remained wide awake until morning, vibrating to the sound track of my marital future, and wondering what my parents would say when they found out that we had eloped.

After the brief ceremony in City Hall, Jim was handed our *livret de famille*—a slim, hand-sewn booklet, with a burgundy, leather-like cover and gold writing. The little book is the record from which all other official records are constructed. It shows not only your current status— who is married to whom—but additional pages are also provided for all future events: births, deaths, everything that affects your civil status. A final, blank, last page titled "*Chronique de famille*" was dedicated to family events outside the official categories. Our pages remained blank, though standing in the office of the deputy mayor, we fully imagined that they would be filled in. Getting married makes you a family. The *livret* is a little book from which you start the official narrative. I was ready.

My friend Hannah, who was doing research for her dissertation in Paris, had come to Geneva by train in order to be our witness at the town's City Hall. In the picture taken by the local photographer, who waited for the couples as they left the official ceremony, we are standing awkwardly on a marble floor in front of a huge symbolist mural, designed to fit the curves and arches of the public space. I am wearing a fitted, dark blue mesh dress and my hair is piled high. My chignon, resembling a small challah, had been braided that morning at the hairdresser and sprayed for eternity. I'm carrying a beige purse and wearing matching beige sling-back pumps. Hannah is wearing a wine-colored suit and a white blouse. Our skirts are knee length, our stockings sheer. Jim stands stiffly between us in a dark three-piece suit. The expression on our faces is as hard to read as the enigmatic smiles of the toga-clad figures in the mural behind us.

After the ceremony, the three of us stopped for an elegant lunch overlooking Lake Geneva, but I spent the entire meal *en crise*, stretched out on the soft leather banquette with intense cramps, occasionally sipping mineral water, while the two of them polished off the champagne and toasted our future.

Hannah took the train back to Paris. Jim and I returned through the mountains. Looking at the snow from the dazzling vistas of the Mont Blanc, Jim sketched our brilliant future. First, we would move to a wonderful apartment with central heating. He would have a language school with the latest techniques developed in America. The school would be so successful, it would have franchises, like Berlitz—or, as long as we were dreaming, Volkswagen. Why not take advantage of what capitalism had to offer, as long as you treated the workers properly? Or he'd sell the idea of the school to some big capitalist, and we'd retire to the countryside on the proceeds of the sale. When I wasn't teaching for him, I would stay home, wash the socks (by then, someone else would be washing the socks), and look after the children. I'd translate famous novels into English and make lots of money, too. The extravagance was Irish, I figured. But as far as I could tell, it worked. He had just signed up three new companies.

Part of my job as *lectrice* at the Sorbonne was to spend several hours a week in the language laboratory, tuning in on students and correcting their pronunciation. I also made tapes for the listening library. That winter, I had been asked to record passages from *Of Mice and Men*. As George and Lennie, the cowboy heroes of the novel, move from job to job, George holds out a vision of the future for Lennie, a comforting story about getting off the road and settling down. They will buy a little place of their own with rabbits, and Lennie will tend the rabbits. Lennie likes George to describe what it's going to be like when they get the ranch. I choked up whenever the rabbits appeared on the page. Whenever Jim talked about the future, I pictured getting the ranch and I choked up.

Like Lennie, I loved hearing the story.

BEFORE LEAVING FOR GENEVA, WE had debated how to tell our families. Since Jim's mother didn't believe in divorce, there was no point in alerting her. Maybe with enough time, she would adjust to the new reality of Jim's unorthodox life when there was no choice about it. He would have to explain it to her in person. I had been very fond of Bernard's mother. What good did that do? She wasn't the person I was going to marry. I wasn't in any hurry to find out if I would like Jim's mother. Nothing he had told me about her pointed in that direction. If she was anything like my father's mother, whom she uncannily resembled in photographs, knowing her would not be an unmitigated pleasure.

Despite their more emancipated airs and their college educations, my parents would say no to the marriage, for Jewish reasons as primitive as the Catholic ones but disguised as secular and pragmatic. My mother couldn't get past the beard. My father was skeptical about Jim's track record as a breadwinner. "You can do better," they had concluded after meeting Jim in Provincetown. That I could do better had been the line since David. I could always do better. Could I?

Jim and I agreed that we should write separately to my parents. I shamelessly began my letter with the cliché, "By the time you receive this letter . . ." And I went on to outline all the many, equally unsatisfactory, ways we could have chosen to apprise them of our desire to marry: a letter from Jim asking permission to marry me; a telegram the day of the wedding itself; getting married in secret and trying to persuade them after the fact, and then, if all discussion were to no avail—announcing it as a fait accompli.

Jim's letter put himself utterly in the wrong, anticipating my parents' concerns, looking ahead to meeting on new terms, and forming a new family. He couldn't now ask permission to marry me, but he would like to ask for their acceptance of the fact of our love and marriage. "Your letter was incredibly stupid," my mother wrote (her default judgment). "Fortunately, Jim's letter was really beautiful." We did not tell them that I had drafted the letter Jim signed.

They were more resigned, finally, than outraged. At least I wasn't moving to North Africa. Jim was presentable. He looked like an academic. Cast in the right tone—"not bad for a first marriage," one of their friends quipped—I had done something impulsive, something romantic that could be folded into an amusing narrative. Once they had absorbed the shock of the elopement, my parents decided to put a good face on the marriage. They ordered engraved wedding announcements for their friends and sent enough biographical details to the newspapers to make us read like a glamorous international couple. Maybe they even believed it.

Vin et Fromage

OUR MARRIAGE HAD BEEN CELEBRATED in the "strictest intimacy," as the phrase on our own wedding announcement worded it. The expression was literally true: only my friend Hannah and the local photographer had witnessed the ceremony in Geneva. When ordinary life resumed in Paris, Jim organized a small wine-and-cheese party in the tiny living room of his apartment, on a Sunday afternoon.

As usual, I cleaned the house, and Jim did the shopping. It took him a week to complete the cheese buying, covering Paris by scooter to hit his favorite neighborhood markets on the right day, planning the purchases so that each cheese had the correct amount of time to reach perfection when served. Jim chose thirty cheeses (most of which he had tasted in their official home, the location that gave them their pedigree—the coveted government seal of authenticity, *appellation contrôlée*) and thirty bottles of wine (same story), each cheese paired with the appropriate wine, and almost as many kinds of bread.

The day of the party, Jim rose especially early and wrote little cards in his neat Catholic school penmanship, identifying the name of every cheese and every wine. The centerpiece of the *vin et fromage* was a ripe Neufchâtel, Coeur de Bray, a cheese from Normandy shaped in the form of a heart paired with a burgundy called Saint-Amour. Jim never could resist a pun. Saint-Amour was the wine he chose to toast our guests.

There were not quite as many guests as cheeses. Jim's old friends, Paul, the French Communist schoolteacher (who had rescued my *navets glacés* from culinary disgrace), and Danh, the Vietnamese philosopher; Hannah; Monique and Alain; Nicole, my friend from Barnard who had married Laurent, a French engineer; Leo; Nathalie from the lycée; Philippe and Anne; Jean and his new wife; and several of the teachers who taught for Jim but were also friends. Thomas and Micheline sent a wall-sized tapa cloth from Tahiti with their regrets. Our social world was still small, even motley, but for the time being, at least, it fit the scale of the apartment. Everyone thought it was very like Jim to have pulled off the cheese-and-wine pairing, even finding cheeses the French friends did not recognize. Sunday afternoons in Paris were gloomy affairs, almost provincial, when everything was closed. The party was seen as a charming interlude, if also, despite all the exotic French cheeses, very American, which of course it was.

AFTER THE SUCCESS OF HIS first letter, Jim started corresponding with my parents on a regular basis. He described the party and the highlights of the honeymoon. I sometimes wondered if he had married me in order to have an audience he took to be knowledgeable enough to appreciate the culture he had acquired, since references to French writers and history and his knowledge of wine and cheese were lost on his family. He narrated our wedding trip back and forth to Geneva, emphasizing its literary stopping points: Langres (birthplace of Diderot) and Morat (where Rousseau had visited). It never occurred to him that my parents weren't as fascinated by the Enlightenment as he was.

The trip's highlight and Jim's secret destination for us—this was not part of the travelogue—was the Issenheim altarpiece in Kolmar. As we stared at the nails embedded in Christ's flesh, the twisted toes dripping blood, Jim reminded me that he had always said he would marry me. Didn't I remember that first day in my room when he promised that he would take me to *l'autel* (altar)? Yes, but I thought he meant *l'hôtel*—as in tryst. Jim's joy in punning was a symptom of his James Joyce obsession. He was especially proud of any pun I missed.

Typically, Jim's letters detailed household activities, made requests—back issues from the *New York Review of Books,* recipes for Jewish dishes—and reported about me, my health, my exams, my shoe shopping. I was the center, the heroine, of this domestic narrative. Sometimes his letters eerily echoed mine, down to the same language—my "elation" after teaching the translation class. He even enclosed examples of the texts I assigned the students to translate— Stendhal, Zola, Camus, Colette. He promoted me to my own parents as a teacher of literature.

Most of all, Jim loved to say "we"; so did I. "We are both very busy, but it's a pretty good life. Once we get a decent apartment, life will be perfect."

The ranch.

Jim had started a campaign to convince my parents of his interest in Judaism. On the envelope of one of his first son-in-law letters to my parents, fat and heavy with the mimeographed pages of my class assignments, are several stamps, one of which represented a column of men with shaven heads, wearing the striped uniforms of the concentration camps, emerging through an archway that resembles the Arc de Triomphe. The men appear to walk through strands of barbed wire, as well as a linked chain. The caption reads: "The return of the deported." The date was April 1965. There had been a ceremony in Père Lachaise cemetery that month to dedicate a monument to the many thousands of the French deportees who died in Buchenwald. It was the anniversary of the liberation of the camp prisoners nineteen years earlier. Like the Chagall stamp of the shtetl betrothal, the liberation stamp carried proof of Jim's desire to feel solidarity with his Jewish family, to identify with Jewish suffering.

I had hoped that in marrying Jim and living with him in Paris, I would escape my nice-Jewish-girl destiny. I longed for glamour and style, Frenchness, Jean Seberg in *Breathless,* or Jeanne Moreau (even more of a reach) playing the Marquise de Merteuil in the movie version of *Les Liaisons Dangereuses.* I had not foreseen *Yiddishkeit* on Hudson transported back to the banks of the Seine. I wanted to travel to Italy, not Israel. Getting married had messed up the geography and collapsed the distances.

The Daube

I FELT AT LEAST AS jubilant as Jane Eyre when she finally married Rochester. There was, I confess, more than a whiff of that heady perfume— wedding the older man who is difficult, moody, who comes with secrets, stamped with something opaque about his past. The older man who after employing you, comes to recognize you as his equal and co-conspirator. Lucy Snowe and Monsieur Paul, the stern schoolteacher. At every chance I stretched out my arm and spread the fingers of my left hand to admire the slenderness of the wedding band we had chosen. In French the gold band is called an *alliance*—I loved that idea, our alliance that I spelled out in a hyphenated last name, linking our ancestors and our destinies. Of course, Brontë doesn't tell us much about what happens *after* her heroines get married. It's not hard to understand why that might be. Except for the adultery plot of continental novels—*Madame Bovary* or *Anna Karenina*—how do you keep the reader's attention with the ordinary details of married existence?

When my parents came to Paris that summer of 1965 on their annual European jaunt, I invited them for dinner along with Monique and Alain, and Monique's parents, who had definitively left Tunisia for Paris. After their disappointment over my breakup with Bernard, Monique and Alain had slowly come to accept Jim as my partner. They had been married for over a year and played old-married couple to our nervous newlywed game. Bringing the two families together was my way of showing my parents I could live the way they did. Was I trying to please them, or worse still, trying to be them?

I decided on a *boeuf en daube* as a main course. I had never cooked a *daube,* but Jim wanted to reenact Woolf's famous portrayal of Mrs. Ramsay's dish in *To the Lighthouse.* Jim liked the idea of French cooking filtered through a literary example, even if English. Literature raised food to a higher level, he said, whatever its national origin.

In *French Provincial Cooking,* Elizabeth David tries to reassure the novice cook by saying that, basically, cooking *en daube* is just like braising. You brown meat on a high heat and put it in a slow oven. "This is an easy recipe," she begins. I took Elizabeth David at her word. After all, I had seen my mother make pot roast many times. Of course I didn't know what rump of beef was (her recommendation) and didn't have an oven. I told the butcher I was making a *daube.* The meat he offered me looked a little fatty. I hesitated, but he insisted that I didn't want meat that would dry out; that's why you also needed cubes of bacon. The meat marinated in a pot on the windowsill overnight (cold enough that July), soaking in a mixture of vinegar, olive oil, some red wine, herbs and vegetables, and a *bouquet garni,* all designed to lend flavor to the meat while it tenderized. The *bouquet* wasn't mentioned by Elizabeth David, but the butcher said it was a good idea and I figured he should know. I was just a *petite dame;* he was the butcher. The next day, I simmered the *daube* on low heat for several hours.

I brought out the dish in a large earthenware terrine, glazed on the inside, as per Elizabeth David's instructions. It looked perfect at the center of our new table. With the wedding present check sent by my aunt and uncle, we had bought a reproduction eighteenth-century Spanish rustic table with sculpted legs and a curved cast-iron base, around the corner on the boulevard Raspail. The mixture of meat, vegetables, and herbs gave off a scent of the French countryside; it gave life to the dark-stained table. I served everyone, ladling the right balance of meat and liquid onto each guest's plate.

The respective parents kept up the conversation in a mixture of French and English—Monique's father speaking English to my father, my mother speaking French to Monique's mother—but a strained silence settled over the table once everyone tackled the *daube,* which in theory should have been tender enough to eat with a spoon. Instead, I heard the work of knives and forks, spearing and trimming the meat on the plate. The chunks of beef had slimmed down to nubs of gristle with a few glimmers of meat attached, a bay leaf floating sadly on the surface of the fatty sauce. My father, who liked fat, tried to console me by saying that the sauce was good, and demonstrated his solidarity by soaking it up with a piece of baguette; my mother offered to send me *her* recipe for *daube.*

I escaped to the kitchen as often as possible, desperate for dishes to wash, but by the end of the meal the disaster of the *daube* had moved into a past tense, mitigated by the salad (I had perfected my vinaigrette), the cheese course, the fruit, and the dessert, not to mention several bottles of very good Burgundy. In a parting gesture, Monique's father toasted us by reciting some of his poetry.

After the guests left, my parents asked us to sit down in the living room with them. My father handed Jim an envelope. It contained a check generous enough for us to buy a car, with the condition, my mother said as she walked out the door, that Jim teach me to drive.

Everyone in *To the Lighthouse* agreed that Mrs. Ramsay's dish was a "perfect triumph." While I finished drying the dessert dishes and the glasses, Jim read aloud the dinner table scene from the novel. In company, Jim had sought to divert attention from my failure by talking up the wine and pushing the cheese course. Alone with me, he couldn't resist the usual critique of my culinary performance, which sadly received a very poor grade. I pointed out that credit for the *daube* masterpiece properly belonged to Mildred, the cook—and also that we didn't have an oven. Still, we had survived the bridal ritual: cooking for the parents.

In London, we bought a dark green Austin-Mini 850 and drove it to Ireland for our delayed honeymoon.

A Soft-Boiled Egg

Jim's cousins found us a cottage on a hilltop looking out at the mountains in the west of Ireland. The cottage had two rooms, the larger of which was a spacious kitchen with a big turf stove and a settee. We had electricity but no running water. The young couple who rented the house to us brought us fresh water and a small sack of potatoes daily. It rained lightly every day, almost invisibly—what the Irish call "soft" weather. We bought heavy cable-knit sweaters, made in the Aran Islands from wool so thick and rich with lanolin it was almost rain resistant, and kept the turf fire burning day and night. I spent most of the day under the quilt reading. Cows circled the cottage, grazing on our rented twelve acres. Sometimes when I got fed up with the sound of their bells, I wrapped myself in a knee rug that I used as a shawl when I went outside and ran around beating pots and pans to make the cows wander off.

That summer, Radio Caroline, a pirate radio station, started broadcasting off the coast of Great Britain, and we listened, ravished, to the Beatles, and to music from America. We took Cher's hit "I Got You Babe" as our anthem.

Green vegetables were scarce, but meat was copiously available. The butcher in town would cut slabs from a large side of meat hanging from a hook above the counter. He would ask how much you wanted and then cut big chunks of whatever part he happened to have under the cleaver. He threw the meat on one side of the scale and individual weights on the other. The method was primitive compared to the minute calculations of the knives and scales in Paris, but the meat, especially the lamb, was fresh. We probably had just seen the donor wandering down the road. In a quest for herbs, we combed our few acres in vain. But there seemed to be an infinite variety of potatoes. Potatoes and onions thrown together with the meat were what the butcher recommended. By the end of the month I turned out a decent Irish stew, consoling myself briefly for the *daube* fiasco.

"THE FLESH IS SAD, ALAS, and I've read all the books." The line of poetry whose authorship we had debated when we met—Mallarmé or Baudelaire?—had become a standing joke. During damp midsummer in Ireland, however, the honeymoon flesh *was* sad, a mute frustration I tried to ignore. Sex with Jim was frequent, but it was shaped by his fantasy, not mine. My fantasies were always about seduction, the man and I were fully clothed and on the verge. The fact that Jim took everything Georges Bataille had written about eroticism to the letter and would urge me to say transgressive things made him—sometimes me— feel daring and modern. Uttering the words didn't necessarily dissolve boundaries or shatter consciousness, which was what Jim, following Bataille's philosophy (maybe you had to be Catholic) seemed to believe. Whatever the philosophy, and even with the example of *Lady Chatterley's Lover*, a novel that had electrified my imagination when I was a virgin in high school, endowing sexual organs with names felt ridiculous off the page.

Thanks to Bernard's tutelage, I could produce the occasional orgasm, but something I never quite named to myself was always missing. Maybe this was what sex in marriage was. After all, the hot sex in *Lady Chatterley's Lover*, like the scenes in the nouvelle vague movies that came later to fuel my curiosity, took place between lovers, not spouses. Clearly, Emma Bovary was looking for something that escaped Charles's imagination. And like Charles, Jim had no clue that anything was wrong.

The act itself often felt like a brutal interruption, especially at dawn. I didn't welcome Jim's morning salute as a tribute to my charms or as proof of his superior virility, as he liked to claim. I didn't know how to get past his complacency, and I worried because my previous encounters had also left me wondering. Was this all there was? When a married friend told me that in her husband's arms it was always like paradise, I was impressed but baffled, and much too embarrassed to ask for details.

IF JIM AND I WERE less world-weary than the depressed poets we both admired, the novelty of running after cows and washing from an outdoor faucet soon passed, and we had literally read all our books. We left our green retreat for a long literary weekend in Dublin. Jim booked a room at a hotel he knew on Dawson Street, around the corner from his tailor and his favorite bookstore—Hodges Figgis, farther down the road.

The room had an en-suite bathroom—for once no bathroom down the hall, no waiting for the neighbor to finish. The hot water came dribbling out in a trickle, but just the act of turning a knob and seeing the tub fill up was almost erotic—good plumbing is pleasure's twin, I had started to think. So what if that made me hopelessly American? The first night, Jim had fallen asleep by the time I emerged bright red from my prolonged soaking in the claw-footed tub. I wrapped myself in the white towels and peered out of the windows at the dark streets. The only lights came from the ornate wrought-iron lampposts.

The next morning we wandered into a cavernous dining room and sat down to a beautifully laid table: a heavy white linen tablecloth, linen napkins, tall crystal water glasses. Breakfast was Jim's favorite meal, and he intended to have a "Full Irish" breakfast. When the waiter asked me what I wanted, I chose what I thought would be simplicity itself. A three-minute boiled egg. Toast. Orange juice. The waiter arrived with Jim's breakfast—fried eggs, fried tomato, blood pudding, fried bacon, all soaking in shining grease—and my solitary egg in a pristine white porcelain cup. I lightly tapped the top of the egg, afraid that too strong a motion would cause the yolk to spurt over the tablecloth. I needn't have worried. The yolk was completely hard, solid yellow. I could have peeled the egg. Jim was halfway through his full plate and the *Irish Times*, but looked up to order another soft-boiled egg.

The waiter shortly returned with a new egg. I tapped the top. The surface crackled slightly. No yellow fluid oozed. I burst into tears. Jim calmly finished his coffee, dabbing at his lips with the napkin and ignoring my tantrum. He would never let a scene ruin a meal. That was the rule of all rules. I could not imagine a meal without a scene. That was how I had grown up: mealtimes were always a battleground. Was it the egg, was it the sex, or were my tears about something else? I had wanted this, this man, this story. Why couldn't he be the way I needed him to be? I wanted to punish Jim for not guessing what I needed and giving it to me without my asking. Part of me knew this wasn't fair.

THE LAST DAY IN DUBLIN, we drove north of the city toward Howth, until we came to a stretch of beach with a stone jetty reaching out into the sea. Jim parked the car and we walked out in silence, watching the waves lap up at the rocks, at the birds landing and taking off along the strand. It was windy and too cold to stand still, but Jim was in a kind of trance.

After a while he asked me if I remembered the scene in *Portrait of the Artist* in which Stephen has the epiphany. I confessed that I had never gotten past the first few pages of the novel, but during my artistic phase in college, I had danced in a theater department version of *Finnegans Wake*. Did that count? When Stephen sees the bird-girl, Jim explained, he realizes that he is not going to become a priest. I had no idea where this was going.

"My mother wanted me to be a priest," Jim said finally, as if relieved of a burden.

I should have felt happy about this confession. Jim almost never told me anything intimate. He expected me to guess his feelings. I shared that desire to turn away from the expected path, the thrill of finding in Paris a world that seemed to keep me at a safe distance from the family that locked me in and that he now adored. Jim offered me extra resistance against that story: marrying him meant marrying out. I looked at his florid complexion, his tight, thin lips, and saw the portrait of his Irish mother, whose photograph he had finally shown me when we got married. We had made our pact on this shared refusal to be our parents' children—but maybe it wasn't shareable. Maybe it wasn't enough.

It was August, but the wind was bitter and my hair was whipping my face. I ran back to the car and lit a cigarette to get warm.

IN THE PHOTOGRAPHS, THE GIRL on her honeymoon is hard to read. She looks uneasy in the landscape, looking toward the sea, a question mark in her eyes. In Jim's favorite picture, I'm crouching outside the cottage doing laundry by hand in a big metal pail and a small plastic basin. That was the snapshot he sent to my parents. Once during that summer, Jim let me take a picture of him without a jacket. Dressed in the cardigan we had just bought but still wearing a shirt and tie, he smiles fully into the camera without the sadness that usually filtered his gaze, happy to be in Ireland.

On our way back to Paris, we stopped in London to stock up on books: Forster, Wilson, Svevo in translation. We were Francophiles, but our reading pleasures still came in English. While we were shopping in Foyle's, our new car was clamped and towed away.

Housekeeping

IN NOVEMBER 1965 A COLD wave swept through France—the lowest temperatures recorded since 1885. The only heating in our tenement was provided by an expensive radiator on wheels that burned oil. We were lucky to get it on special, the man in the hardware store had said, when he saw Jim's hesitation. The heater worked remarkably well in the small space, except during the coldest weather when I retreated to bed. Wrapped in my Irish knee rug, I would sit under the covers with the radiator rolled up next to me, grading papers from my translation class and smoking Mecarillos. I liked thinking about George Sand, the only woman I knew of who had smoked cigars. The little cigars were hard to get used to, but I thought I might smoke less if I smoked cigars, particularly without inhaling. Alternatively, I hoped that I'd become a writer someday, not just a grader of student translations.

One Sunday morning Jim and I woke up early, coughing. The air in the bedroom was fogged with soot rising from the sputtering heater.

Jim grabbed my heavy winter coat and wrapped me in it. I pulled on my boots, still dressed in my nightgown. Jim covered his mouth and nose with his handkerchief, turned off the heater, flung open the bedroom windows, and dragged me out of the apartment. We climbed on his scooter that was parked out front and headed for the Bois de Bou-logne to breathe fresh air. I clung to Jim's back as he sped through the empty streets.

In the black-and-white photographs Jim took of me that day, I look like one of those reckless women in Antonioni movies in which the heroine has gone to the edge of an emotional abyss, dazed and pained—her face blank and drained of emotion at the end of a long night. We could have suffocated, we told friends when we dined out. Jim, who had decided to document every aspect of our life together, brandished the pictures of my appearance that day as proof. He was proud of having captured my pallor.

The near-death episode with the oil heater finally persuaded Jim that it was time to leave Montparnasse. I found an apartment in a brand-new building located in the unfashionable tenth arrondissement around the Gare de l'Est, and we moved in just before Christmas. The eleven-story apartment house, around the corner from the train sta-tion, was set back in a cul-de-sac, flanked by small textile factories that looked as though they were going out of business at any moment. Like most modern construction going up in Paris, the apartment building was made of concrete, not the noble *pierre de taille* that gave the city its characteristic look of elegance. Adorned only by cast-iron grids, from which some tenants, hoping to impart a personal touch to their anony-mous dwelling, had hung flowerpots with geraniums, the façade rivaled the dismal look of the HLMs, the low-income housing projects subsi-dized by the government. From our ninth-floor perch, though, we had a view of Parisian rooftops, with the dome of Sacré-Coeur in the far distance. I liked seeing the landmark from my window—another icon of my chosen destination.

Except for the Canal Saint-Martin—and even it was discourag-ingly seedy—the neighborhood, we were forced to admit, lacked charm. At night, for consolation, we sometimes went for walks along the canal, always stopping at the spot where, in the movie *Hôtel du Nord*, the great actress Arletty, standing on a little footbridge, utters the famous line of sublime indignation to Louis Jouvet, who thinks he can get away with saying that he's leaving town (her) because he needs a change of scene: "Atmosphère? Moi, atmosphère!" A decrepit Hôtel du Nord was still standing on the far side of the canal, visible from the bridge, but the movie hadn't been shot on location, I was crushed to discover after perfecting my Arletty imitation.

The shoddy architecture and the shabby surroundings made it possible for us to afford a miniscule two-bedroom apartment. The so-called second bedroom was no more than a tiny passageway, presumably designed for an infant. In the meantime, Jim would make the space his office. The glossy wood floors were warm from central heating. I walked around in bare feet again. But the bathroom alone, I explained to French friends who couldn't fathom how we could have left Montparnasse for the Gare de l'Est, made up for the neighborhood. Only Americans, they said, could care that much about plumbing.

WITH A NEWLY INSTALLED HALF-SIZE refrigerator in the kitchen, I launched into a full-scale French housewife impersonation. Always dressed as though I were going to teach, always in a dress, I would take my woven straw basket to the Saint-Quentin covered market a few blocks away and wander through the array of stalls. After several weeks of cruising, I chose my people, crucially the *maraîcher*, a tiny old man who made me feel that I had a chance of passing. After I pointed to the head of lettuce I had chosen, the vegetable man would wrap the leaves, heavy with sandy dirt and the occasional slug, in newspaper that I then carefully placed on top of the vegetables in my straw basket. Every time, the vegetable man asked me if I knew how to make a salad dressing, and every time he reminded me how to make it: lemon juice and olive oil blended together with the tiniest hint of mustard. I was always especially gratified when my choice—pale soft *laitue* or crispier *batavia*, depending on the season—was rewarded by the offer of "un peu de persil, madame?" It became a point of honor with me never to pay for an entire bunch of parsley when I needed only a few sprigs. I learned how to make the ritualistic conversation that constituted a requirement for being served correctly. The vegetable sellers were pedagogues in their own right, never letting you choose your own melon or tomatoes. They alone would adjudicate. When is the melon for, madame, or even what time of day? Ripeness calibrated to the hour.

I secretly vibrated to being called "madame," although I also worried about being old, the strands of gray hair that I covered with henna. I wanted to be an adult, but what was supposed to happen to a woman after she got married? The movies that had nourished me did not point in the direction of groceries. The only thing Jean Seberg seemed to shop for (besides the Dior dress, of course) was a Renoir reproduction of a young woman in profile to tack up on her hotel room walls.

At the huge Prisunic on Champs-Élysées, a mini–department store that sold home furnishings in addition to almost everything else, we bought, at prices suggested by the name, inexpensive Italian pieces made of wooden slats and foam rubber cushions—a loveseat and chairs—that you assembled yourself. But the heart of the living room furniture was a solid, cherrywood bookcase we found that worked with floor-to-ceiling poles and combined our books. I loved the long shelves of books that looked like the beginning of a serious library.

Now that there was an actual bathroom, toilet, and kitchen, someone had to assume the job of cleaning it all. Jim considered the household work the woman's responsibility. I thought so too, but once we had married, I didn't seem to want to do it anymore. My initial enthusiasm for floor washing had begun to wane. A few weeks after we moved in, I found Aysha, who worked for the neighbor across the hall. I shared the news with my mother: "I now have a *femme de ménage*: a woman from North Africa. She spent yesterday and today scrubbing the toilet and kitchen and is starting on the bathroom today. The walls were black and she did a great job." Aysha had showed up the first morning with a bucket and a *serpillière,* a thick, absorbent cloth for mopping. She poured large amounts of water all over the floor and went down on hands and knees, flicking the edges of the dampened cloth against the floorboards. I had seen women wash this way in Tunisia, where the floors were tiled. Were you supposed to put all that water on wood? I couldn't bring myself to ask the question—presumably this is what she did for the neighbor—but I was mortified to have a woman on her hands and knees in my apartment, even if, in emulation of my mother, who always insisted on her right to have "help" whether or not she was working, I assumed it was normal for another woman to do the housework I didn't want to do.

One evening, a few weeks after Aysha started cleaning the apartment, I was unable to turn on the lights in the entry when I returned home from work. I frantically dialed SOS Réparations. An electrician arrived within the hour carrying his toolbox and a meter. It turned out that the electrical circuits, insufficiently protected by the brand-new floorboards, had been drowned by Aysha's watery zeal. The repairman fell to work. I watched him mutely, mesmerized by the ticking, like the meter of a taxi stuck in traffic. The francs kept adding up.

"You have to let the wiring dry for a couple of days," the electrician said three hours later when he had finished. "Next time buy a vacuum cleaner. It's cheaper," he volunteered sympathetically.

SOON AFTER THE SOS FIASCO, around my birthday in February, I sent my parents one of my stocktaking accounts. These lyrical narratives, which I volunteered periodically, were part of an elaborate strategy of self-justification; the endlessly proliferating demands of domestic life supplied a conflict-free zone of epistolary material. There was something reassuring about sharing the concrete facts of daily existence that served as a buffer against my persistent uncertainty about what I was supposed to be doing in my life that moving continents had aggravated rather than assuaged. "I'm cooking up a storm, French and Jewish, rabbit with mushrooms and white wine and stuffed cabbage. Farfel (Jim's passion). Planning to make your daube recipe soon." (Clearly, there was no escaping the *daube*.)

It was as though, after loudly announcing how completely I had left my parents behind, I willingly set out to replicate their life. After much back-and-forth, and returning an illustrated questionnaire my mother had designed, I succeeded in getting her to make curtains for the new apartment, "exactly the same ones," I stipulated, hanging in their living room in Manhattan. We didn't need curtains for privacy—we had no neighbors staring at us from across the street—and all the apartments came fitted with folding metal shutters. But curtains were essential to a certain idea of a living room, my mother thought.

PART OF ME—THE COOKING AND curtains part—wanted to be like my parents. Of course, my parents, like their own, were also trying to be other people. My mother's father wanted only to be a Yankee; he even voted Republican. For my parents, becoming the Americans they wanted to be took the form of disparaging others. My mother managed to find something wrong with everyone, except for a chosen few who all seemed to live on the Upper East Side and whom she envied. Finding the fault—and once named, the fault could never be forgotten—was her strategy for tamping down the intractable anxiety about who she was, who we were as a family, a survival mechanism that they had passed on to me. What else was that constant doubt that kept me twisted in my gut?

"Our anniversary is coming up soon," I wrote in early April, radiating pride. "But unfortunately this year it will be a working day—until 9 p.m.! It's all so unreal. I really think I made a good choice—the right decision." I had learned to drive and acquired another degree. I taught at the Sorbonne, earned my own money. But having chosen Jim and establishing a household of my own were what finally made me a grown-up.

I wanted to prove them wrong about me, even more than I wanted their approval. They could finally talk about me to their friends without shame.

I had inherited my parents' tendency toward condescension, which was matched, if not surpassed, by my new husband's. "Jim and I find most people basically a waste of time," I declared from the height of my bridal sublime. "So many people are pleasant to spend time with but it's as bad as watching television. You get so little from it. There are some exceptions, but very few. And then, Jim resents women who don't cook as well as I do, so that limits dinner invitations. We dread being invited back! (The other night we were served meatballs and spaghetti!) The meal ended with packaged supermarket cheese with the price still on it." Jim refused to continue having dinner with those friends of mine who had committed, he insisted angrily, a veritable crime against cheese—buying it packaged at the supermarket and serving it cold. Cold! Becoming French required getting the food exactly right, down to the rind.

When my parents visited us in Paris that summer, we gave them our bedroom and slept on air mattresses. In a snapshot my father took of my mother and me at the Saint-Quentin market, the two of us are contemplating a small mountain of oranges and grapefruits. I'm wearing my Irish cardigan and carrying my woven straw basket over my arm. My mother is rummaging in her purse for change. We look like matching housewives, except for my mother's silvery hair.

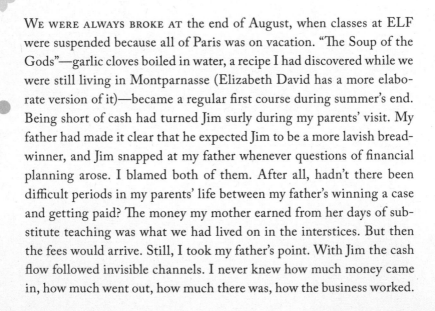

Follow the Money

We were always broke at the end of August, when classes at ELF were suspended because all of Paris was on vacation. "The Soup of the Gods"—garlic cloves boiled in water, a recipe I had discovered while we were still living in Montparnasse (Elizabeth David has a more elaborate version of it)—became a regular first course during summer's end. Being short of cash had turned Jim surly during my parents' visit. My father had made it clear that he expected Jim to be a more lavish breadwinner, and Jim snapped at my father whenever questions of financial planning arose. I blamed both of them. After all, hadn't there been difficult periods in my parents' life between my father's winning a case and getting paid? The money my mother earned from her days of substitute teaching was what we had lived on in the interstices. But then the fees would arrive. Still, I took my father's point. With Jim the cash flow followed invisible channels. I never knew how much money came in, how much went out, how much there was, how the business worked.

His desk was as messy as my father's, and he procrastinated like my father, but that had not yet produced anything resembling my father's success. Could you run a business from the scraps of paper in your back pocket? That was Jim's gamble.

That summer, I stopped drawing a salary from the French government. My teaching contract with the Sorbonne had expired in June and I decided that I had to earn money independently of Jim's school. I was nervous about waiting for things to work out at the ranch. Sometimes I felt I was losing faith in the ranch altogether.

Early in September Jacques Couderc, one of the senior professors at the Sorbonne's Institute for American Studies, described an editorial project to me and Mark Rothberg. Like me, Mark had taught as a lecturer, and Couderc thought we'd make a good team. He wanted us to provide an American version of a book he was putting together for a French audience. He had traveled to the States and interviewed a star lineup of writers. The anthology would be a tapestry of excerpts from some forty American authors—Ellison, Mailer, Baldwin—that he had loosely stitched together with commentary and interviews, showing how contemporary American writers grappled with questions of identity. Since there were no footnotes, quotation marks, or indications of what he had excerpted, our task was to track everything down, working backward from the French translations. As translators, we would get to write our own preface. Of course, we weren't translators—unless finding the original for the translating could be called translating—but Couderc took the view that he knew more about American literature than we did since he had studied it for twenty years, so we couldn't be called editors. Besides, we were translating his introduction.

Mark was planning to apply to a PhD program when he went back to the States, and he was convinced that Couderc possessed the keys to the academic kingdom he wanted to belong to. He urged me to sign on with the project. Couderc promised us royalties, in addition to the equivalent of $1,500 on delivery of the manuscript, and we concluded that the book would be good for our respective futures as academics—if we had futures.

JIM THOUGHT COUDERC WAS USING us, especially me; he was sure Couderc wanted to get into my pants, as he liked to put it. Jim didn't care about my spending time with Mark, of whom he was only occupationally jealous, as he was of all my male friends, even though I had told him I was pretty sure Mark was homosexual. Jim maintained that Couderc was an operator and not a true intellectual, the kind of academic who would do anything to get quoted in *Le Monde* and interviewed on the radio. Naturally, Jim also resented the fact that I was investing my time on someone else's project, instead of devoting myself to making the school happen: working for him! Still, Couderc needed us and we needed money. We would finish the book the following summer before Mark returned to the States. He could tie up any loose ends there; I would deal with Couderc in Paris. We sealed our partnership with a drink at the Select, not far from Mark's hotel on the rue Delambre.

Jim wasn't completely wrong about the sleaze factor. When Mark and I initially discussed the USA project, as we referred to it, we went to Couderc's apartment near the Jardin des Plantes for a drink. He insisted that working for him would put us on the academic map as he had already done with a rapidly rising critic and writer. He led us into the bedroom, opened the American-style closets he had had built in, and proudly showed us the wardrobe—rows of dresses and shoes, neatly lined up according to season and style—of the famous French woman writer whom he claimed to have transformed from a dowdy housewife living in the south of France to a sophisticated *parisienne*.

I defended the USA project to Jim, but I did not tell him about the closet full of shoes.

Meeting Roland Barthes

INSIDIOUSLY, MARK'S ACADEMIC AMBITION WHETTED mine. I decided to get a doctorate in France. What another degree would mean for my ability to earn money was not entirely clear, but going to the next academic level was a Jewish way of moving into the future that felt familiar and comfortable.

I wanted to write a thesis on Boris Vian, a fashionably marginal but notorious French writer whose work I loved. Vian had died tragically young of a heart attack in 1959, while watching the botched movie version of his novel *I'll Spit on Your Graves*—a fake translation from the American. Vian had been fascinated by the mythological America that French people had created for their own satisfaction: jazz, Negroes, hard-boiled detectives. I wanted to study his translations of American crime writers—James Cain and Raymond Chandler—whose books had appeared in the *Série noire*, the French crime series Gallimard began publishing right after the war. But no sooner had I officially registered my subject than an American professor of French published a study on Vian, introducing him to an American audience. I would have to expand my original interest in Vian's work to a broader project, an analysis of all the American detective novels translated in the French series.

I worked up the courage to present my topic to Roland Barthes, the literary critic famous for his brilliant analyses of cultural myths. He received me during his regular office hours. He sat at a distance, leaning away from his desk—an old, long, elegant wood table—looking past me at the view outside his window.

"What can I do for you, madame?" he asked, bored, or maybe just languorous, yet polite. He looked at me as though he might have seen me before—one of those mute presences filling seats in his overflowing seminar that I had been attending at the school of Hautes Études, where he was director of studies. I told him I was sitting in on his seminar. Barthes nodded briefly, politely, and looked past me again out the window. I explained that I wanted to study the translations of the first books in the *Série noire*. The translations made the tough-guy world more violent than it already is, as if to produce an image of America that flatters the French worldview. The French have culture, I concluded, pleased with my idea, Americans, anti-culture. It's all about language.

Barthes crossed and uncrossed his pale hands, which he held clasped on the table.

"That might be interesting," he said finally, lighting another cigarette. "I'll have to trust you," he added with his famous half-smile that seemed to forgive my blatant parroting of his latest work, "on the nuances in English."

As Jim pointed out in Educating the Parents, his weekly letter to my mother and father, my idea about language as content was in fact wholly indebted to Barthes, whom he likened to his hero, the Canadian cultural critic Marshall McLuhan, so they would have a North American analogue. This was probably more information than they needed.

I had no idea how to write a thesis; Jim didn't either. The only person I knew working on a dissertation was Hannah, and she had returned to New Haven after completing her research in Paris. But Hannah was getting a degree in history; her bibliography was already longer than anything I had ever written. I hadn't written anything since my master's essay on Laclos and women. I had trouble imagining the leap from the protective arms of American standards, even with my lecherous tutor, into the egregiously hands-off approach of the French professoriate. Once they signed your application for a topic, you were on your own.

After visiting us in Paris, one of Jim's best American friends, whom we always called by his initials, and who was the son of a famous writer, wrote me a two-page, single-spaced, six-point letter about how to write a dissertation. I hadn't asked for his advice, but I must have seemed in need of it. Having spent years on an unpublishable dissertation, and not acknowledging that being the Son of a World Famous Writer (you could feel the capitals like an uncomfortable jacket he wore, too tight) might have something to do with his failure, he sent his guide to thesis writing. The most important thing, he concluded in his final point, was to be sure that the topic mattered to me "personally and emotionally," and that it was important to me generally, within my "spiritual economy."

I wasn't sure I had a spiritual economy. Maybe I would find one along the way.

The Ranch

I HAD BECOME THE GOOD daughter. Granted, Jim was not your dream husband—older, not Jewish, divorced—but the glamour of Paris, and the assumption that things were different, less conventional "over there," added a cachet that seemed to balance, if not entirely cancel, the obvious negatives of my choice. Despite its foreign location, my little rebellion had been integrated by my parents into a safe domestic model.

Back in New York, my younger sister Andrea had assumed the position of the bad daughter. She had moved outside the bourgeois borders of the Upper West Side to the bohemian grunge of the East Village. Taking reverse immigration literally, she headed to the zones of the Lower East Side where my paternal grandparents had started out. My sister had fallen in love with a person so unsuitable in my parents' eyes—"a Puerto-Rican-Negro drop-out," as my father put it—that all my past boyfriends and present husband combined now appeared closely related to Prince Charming. My parents were in shock. If I was still tethered as they were to the values of the 1950s, my sister had already migrated into the 1960s.

My father wrote to us angrily to express his outrage that Jim and I both seemed to approve of my sister's choice:

> *From drop-out to record salesman and now to waiter in a jazz dive. He hasn't a skill nor education. And he is too small to become a policeman or fireman. What kind of future is in store for him? What possible happiness can result from a union with such a boy?*
>
> *If this boy were white and Jewish he would still be all wrong.*
>
> *We strove to educate her for independence and made some small progress. So with the arrogance (displayed ever since she left here) she surrenders her most precious asset—her independence. She can be dumped at a moment's notice.*

Jim and I had tried to defend my sister or at least point out to my parents the weakness of their arguments. Independence, the key to their mythology of parenthood, meant wanting their children to want *their* life. It did not include living it in one room in a bad neighborhood with "such a boy," too short to become a policeman or fireman (my father was being thorough in his catalogue of defects). But what if that's what *she* meant by independence?

My parents were caught in a drama in some ways of their own making, but the family story was shaped by a much larger transformation of urban life. Unlike their friends, who in the 1950s had moved to the suburbs, my parents stayed put in Manhattan and sent us to public school. At Booker T. Washington Junior High School, located at 108th Street and Amsterdam Avenue, we met Irish kids and Puerto Ricans who lived in tenements on the east (wrong) side of Broadway. We learned to dance the cha-cha and the mambo in gym, where all the students came together. The white kids did it by the numbers, counting each step, while the Puerto Rican pupils snickered openly at our pitiful performance. In assembly, we heard about education and democracy

and, by my sister's time, in Social Studies about segregation and inte-
gration. My sister took the lessons in democracy to the letter. If all people were the same, had the same rights, then all people were acceptable
playmates and ultimately, as she saw it, soul mates.

Meanwhile, Jim and I were getting closer to the ranch. As a favor to
my parents, their old acquaintance Jean, Philippe's pal, with whom Jim
and I sometimes socialized, had found us a place where Jim could have
a base of operations for ELF and where we could also live. Out of the
blue one evening when we were all having dinner, Jean offered us a long-
term lease on a large apartment in a fabulous location near the Stock
Exchange. We pitched the idea to my parents who, we hoped, would
be willing to supply the five thousand dollars for the *pas de porte*, the
key money required to take over the lease from the previous tenant. Jim
sketched out the floor plans and enclosed them in a letter to my parents
so they could begin to visualize their investment. They were convinced
by the blueprint for redesigning the apartment from a shop where leather
bindings for books had been made by hand into a language school. Think
of all the money we had saved them by eloping! Wasn't this a much better deal? Their money made our fantasies concrete and official through a
financial compact sealed by a lease and approved by a notary. (In France,
the notary—not the lawyer or the agent—is the ultimate middleman
without whom nothing official can take place.) We were entering the
royal road to the epicenter of high bourgeois culture: real estate.

This time, it really was the ranch. This was what we had talked
about endlessly—how it would be, how it could be, if only. "Jim could
have a secretary and office—a language lab—a classroom in the *center*
of Paris! In terms of living space for us, it would be about the same
with the difference that the study wouldn't exist, but it won't be necessary if Jim has an office. And until we have a child, the small room
at the end could be a study for me. We would miss the view, but you
can't have everything."

You can't have everything.

Of course I would give up my study to make it a child's room.

In America, all my friends were having babies. Not having children meant, Judy wrote in one of her chiding letters, that you weren't

"delivering," as she put it, as a woman. I wasn't sure I believed that, but I stopped taking the pill. After so many years of fearing I was pregnant, I was amazed now not to be, now that I was prepared for it to happen. "No news on the family scene," I informed my parents. Dr. Hirsch said he was sure there was nothing wrong, but we would explore the situation.

The Carpenter

ONE AFTERNOON, LEO INTRODUCED US to Hans, a carpenter who was experienced at renovations. Leo had found a huge empty space near Les Halles that Hans had turned into a beautiful loft. Hans was German, and had come to Paris with his Swedish girlfriend Ingrid, who worked as an au pair for a rich American family.

Jim took Hans through the apartment and showed him what he had in mind. Hans had a theory for every aspect of the renovation. Jim accepted the need to knock down walls in order to create new spaces for the school that would occupy the front end of the apartment. But why dismantle the floor in the back? It was just for us. Hans insisted on taking up all the boards, examining each one, ordering new pieces, and refitting them one by one.

"It's all connected," Hans said, shaking his head, when Jim said he wanted just to patch up the broken floorboards and put throw rugs over the bad spots.

"No one will know the difference."

"I will know," Hans replied, with a slight accent. Leo had warned Jim that Hans was not an ordinary carpenter. Jim was beginning to discover what that meant. After Leo and Hans left, Jim announced that I would oversee the work on the new apartment while he concentrated on developing the school. The division of labor made a kind of sense, despite the fact that I knew nothing about renovation.

I gave myself over to supervising the work in the apartment and abandoned the idea of writing a dissertation. I had wanted the ranch. Maybe this was just as important as writing something no one would read anyhow. Maybe this is what the son of the famous writer meant by my "spiritual economy." It was hard to know. "Somehow life is simplified," I wrote home, "since it is impossible to clean and people are constantly coming in and out. Everything is necessarily casual. I spend half my time in dungarees." I made lunch for Hans, the carpenter, and his helper, but I told them I wanted to be more useful. Reluctantly, Hans assigned me the task of scraping the layers of old wallpaper between the beams in the long corridor that formed the entranceway. When I finished a section of the wall, I'd go find him at the other end of the apartment so that he could see the progress I was making. While I waited for him to come to my end of the apartment, I would dip my scraper in one of the buckets filled with water he always kept near him for the plaster and for rinsing brushes. I loved watching how carefully he took care of his tools. One day, Hans started calling me his "little fish." I had told him I was a Pisces. He said he was an Aquarius. I found myself checking the horoscope.

Hans worked slowly. He explained to Jim that he could go faster, but that would just be a cosmetic job. You'd be satisfied at first, but you'd only have compounded the problem by hiding it. His theory about painting, for instance, was that if you prepared the base properly, opening all the cracks as far as you could, filling them in, sanding, and re-sanding, and created the right foundation, the walls would not just hold the paint but *embrace* it. The walls would glow instead of shine, especially with a lacquer finish, which was what he had chosen for the kitchen. I defended Hans's progress to Jim, who couldn't fathom why it was taking him so long to complete the painting, or why I was scraping wallpaper in the hallway, which was the helper's job.

Jim told my parents that I was overindulging the workers.

"They're really like teenage children," he complained, objecting to their hours and their music.

You Are Killing Me

ONE AFTERNOON IN EARLY FALL I accompanied Hans to the Bazar de l'Hôtel de Ville, the huge department store on the rue de Rivoli that specialized in home furnishings. It was time to choose new wallpaper for the apartment and Hans said that the BHV, as everyone referred to it, had the best selection of patterns. Turning the pages of the sample books together, our faces almost touching, I realized with a shock that I had been falling all over the man Jim had hired to renovate our apartment, stumbling into him as though pushed by a crowd, trying to inch closer and closer to his body.

"The patterns are making me dizzy," I said, almost to myself, putting my hand to my throat. "I have to leave."

Hans steered me by the elbow through the labyrinthine aisles of stacked wallpaper rolls toward the *sortie*. When we finally exited from the BHV, he sat me down at the closest café table.

I stared mutely at Hans's face, as if I were seeing it for the first time. He had the head of the man the heroine in Harlequin romances always falls for. All bones and hollows, sculpted lips, blue eyes deeply set in their sockets, fringy black lashes. Seated at the table, Hans appeared slight, even delicate, but I had seen him lift rafters, floorboards, and sacks of plaster at the apartment without straining. I thought he resembled Horst Buchholz (a.k.a. the German James Dean) in *The Magnificent Seven,* one of the few American movies David would have admitted to admiring, probably because it was a remake of *The Seven Samurai.*

We both ordered coffee and smoked in silence until the waiter reappeared at the table.

I observed his strong, graceful hands, which could fix almost anything, as he slowly stirred sugar into his espresso. Hans waited for me to speak.

"Did you see anything you liked?" I asked, jolted back to the official script by the bitter taste of the coffee.

"It's up to you," Hans said, with his characteristic mixture of deference and irony.

I was flirting in that silly-woman-who-spends-her-husband's-money mode that I had begun to adopt with the workers over whom I felt no authority. I wanted to be one of the kids, not married to the boss. I reached out impulsively and took Hans's hand. He looked surprised but did not withdraw his hand. I could feel a question rising to my lips. It had nothing to do with wallpaper. As I rehearsed the question in my mind, I knew I was flushing.

"Why don't you come to the old place tomorrow night for dinner after work?" I finally found myself saying. "Jim will be out of town," I added, answering his quizzical look. I had met his girlfriend, Ingrid, who sometimes came to pick him up at the end of the day. She was tall—taller than he was—and the Nordic type that appealed to the French. She had come to Paris with Hans from Germany on a student visa and was working as an au pair. She seemed kind.

After a long pause, as if calculating the losses and gains to his job situation, Hans shrugged and said he would come at eight, since the heavy *travaux* of renovation were not allowed after that hour. Jim paid by the hour and was fanatic about a full workday. Hans didn't mention Ingrid and neither did I.

I bought some *plats cuisinés* at the charcuterie near the train station and set them out on the Spanish table in the living room. At the ranch, I cooked for Hans and his helper. Away from the chaos of renovation, I wanted to shed the kitchen image. I was trying for something more worldly, less domestic: more *femme du monde*, less *femme d'intérieur*. Waiting for Hans to arrive, I checked myself in the mirror several times and saw a cliché.

I frantically cleaned the apartment several times to distract myself from the fear that Hans would have a change of heart. What could I do if he didn't come? I could hardly force him to want me. I could ask Jim to fire him (maybe he knew that), but what I longed for was this: I imagined his hands—hands I had watched at work for hours—touching me. I would be the plaster.

I was still looking in the mirror when Hans knocked. I quickly closed the door behind him and leaned against it, the way the woman always does in the movie when she's passionate, blocking the exit. While we were still in the entryway, I reached up for his face, touched his cheek, the chisel of his lips with my fingers. He caught my hand and pulled me toward him. A rush came over me, a strange mixture of adrenaline and languor radiating through every part of my body. Just standing close to Hans I felt liquefied, as I had at the BHV. I wanted to pour my body over his. Lava. I led him by the hand, past the food arrayed on the table, straight through Jim's office into the bedroom, pulling him after me, like a child.

Making love removed all the abstract questions about desire, whether I was capable of feeling it, the puzzle behind the oblique conversations with Monique. "You were made for being caressed," he would say, smiling. A woman in one of Colette's novel comments to another on a lover's technique: "You couldn't do it better yourself." Hans would immobilize me with his hands and mouth, then with an unexpected shift of position push me over the edge. How could he have known just when to make the move, when I didn't? He knew, though, because he always looked at me with a sweet complacency when I finally stopped shuddering. Sometimes I'd feel guilty about receiving so much pleasure with no return, but that was how he seemed to want it most of the time. Over and over again, as though that was all he wanted to say or do, he created a circuit of ecstasy that I had only read about or guessed at from the movies in my repertoire.

Whenever Hans said with his slight accent, "It feels so good. It feels so good to touch you," I would think, finally, yes, it feels so good, I don't know where I am anymore. I'm leaving home, really going somewhere. Lying next to Hans felt like a foreign film. This time I was reliving *Hiroshima Mon Amour*. The movie imprinted on me from its opening shots when you see two bodies—but at first you don't know you are looking at bodies, just sandy shapes, curved forms moving slowly, moving together. At the same time, you hear two voices speaking to each other. The woman is French and the man is Japanese but he is speaking French, slowly, as if he hadn't mastered the language, pausing between words, giving equal weight to each syllable: "Tu n'as rien vu à Hiroshima." The woman's voice says quietly, "Tu me tues. Tu me fais du bien." You are killing me; you are making me feel good. You are good for me. When I watched the movie with David in New York, I did not understand what that meant: "You are killing me; you are making me feel good." How could being killed be good? I was afraid to ask David since the dialogue was what he hated most about the movie.

Suddenly, I thought, yes, kill me, please. You. Of course, to make a movie work for me, I had to bracket what didn't fit, including catastrophes of world history. But I didn't need a whole script, just a point of departure, two people who don't belong together. *Hiroshima Mon Amour* was mainly about heat and skin. A conflagration.

My skin was on fire, and I was all skin.

The Carpenter
and the Lady

WHEN HANS WAS WORKING IN the new space and I was playing helper, I would press myself tightly against his chest the minute Jim left for teaching. We would resist as long as we could, holding in our breath, leaning into each other in a kind of game, kissing, grinding our bodies in the doorways, tempting each other until we gave in and went to lie down in the back room, always keeping an ear open for footsteps. The room was at the opposite end of the horseshoe-shaped apartment, but the front door slammed loud enough for us to hear people coming and going. I finally asked Joe, Hans's helper, to call out when Jim came home.

We never actually made love in the little room, but we often took off our shirts so that our bodies could touch. Once Jim came home unexpectedly early and I pulled on Hans's sweater by mistake. Hans swiftly tucked his tee shirt into his jeans and we hurried out to meet Jim. He looked at us askance, criticizing Hans for not being at work on the beams in the front part of the apartment, and me for not supervising the renovation. It wasn't his fault, I said. I had asked him to see about building me a desk.

"What's wrong with the dining room table?" Jim asked in the exasperated tone that had come to characterize our exchanges since work on the apartment had begun, right after my parents' summer visit. From the beginning of our relationship, Jim would never admit to worry about financial matters or about his chances of success, but over the last months his mood had radiated tension, and I absorbed it daily as the renovations dragged on. This shared but unspoken anxiety, combined with the repeated failure of my attempts to get pregnant, embittered our life together.

I was caught in two interlocking triangles, Jim, my parents, and me, and Jim, Hans, and me. The figures did not belong to the same geometry, but they expressed the same problem. My parents had provided serious key money, and had it not been for their fancy connections, we would never have found our fabulous address. I was now newly indebted to them and, at the same time, committed both to the marriage and to making the school dream come into being, thus justifying my parents' investment in us. It was easier to quarrel with Jim over the renovation dramas than to confront the emotional abyss we were circling in our very expensive space.

The sweater was inside out and I knew I was flushed, my face red from rubbing against the edges of Hans's sharp stubble. I could feel Jim's eyes studying the seams of the sweater.

Jim said nothing. I wasn't sure what he was thinking, but I knew he was much too enamored of our intellectual bond to imagine me having an affair with a carpenter he paid ten francs an hour, however "artistic," as he put it when he wrote to my parents to report on the progress of the renovations. Snobbery was on my side.

I felt like a prisoner waiting for the jailer to leave in order to exercise a furtive pleasure within my cell. I yearned to be alone with Hans without the anxiety of interruption. We were paying rent on the old apartment, but Jim still went there occasionally to pack up his remaining books. I would have loved to take Hans to the Pont-Royal, where I had

spent an afternoon with Jonathan. Or bring him late one night to the legendary Grand Véfour around the corner for a romantic *souper,* sitting in
a deep booth, thinking of famous lovers in history whose stories figured
in the nameplates above the booths. I missed the borrowed comfort of
luxurious settings. Instead, we walked over to the rue Saint-Denis, near
the huge food market, Les Halles, where prostitutes worked the streets
day and night. Hans was initially shocked by my solution. I agreed that
it was kind of creepy (*déclassé* was the word that came to mind—but I
couldn't use that word with him). In the end, I was *la patronne*—who was
he to disagree?

　The rue Saint-Denis was lined with seedy hotels and bars, bistros
open late at night and early in the morning for the workers from the
market as well as the prostitutes and their customers. *Les filles,* blonde
hair teased high on their heads and cascading down the sides in imitation of Brigitte Bardot, perched on stiletto-heeled pointy-toed shoes
or boots, their legs exposed under miniskirts, leaned provocatively in
the doorways and in front of the hotels. They called out to the men
passing by, inviting them with their eyes, bodies, and words: "Tu viens?
Tu m'amènes?" Some of the men walked right past the girls looking
straight ahead or hanging their heads, the married ones, presumably, as
if they hoped not to be seen (but by whom would they be seen if not by
someone equally guilty?); the bolder ones overtly cruised the merchan-
dise. In a flash, a decision would be taken, a sum decided upon, and the
couple would vanish from the sidewalk.

　I finally chose the Saint-Denis because it looked like the Hôtel
du Nord. At the reception desk, we had to show our passports (police
checks were universal), but when we paid cash, without a second glance
we were given a room and a key—the old-fashioned kind with the long
stem and big brass marker. We walked up the stairs and saw other couples coming down. It was just a hotel, after all, even if rooms rented by
the hour.

　The room was sparsely furnished and lacking in charm, but the
sheets didn't appear soiled. The sink had taps with hot and cold water,
as did the bidet; the toilet was down the hall. So, no, it wasn't the Pont-
Royal, but privacy was the luxury we craved. Besides, we were used to

touching while still covered with the sawdust of the apartment, finger-nails spotted with paint, skin pale gray with plaster. The first hour we barely moved, exhausted from getting ourselves onto a bed behind locked doors. We lay there quietly, breathing each other in.

I wondered fleetingly if D.H. Lawrence was right, after all: intel-lectual women think too much for their own pleasure. The lyrics of "If I Were a Carpenter and You Were a Lady" ran around the borders of my brain. I tried to resist the banality of the categories, but he *was* a carpenter, and I was, at least in comparison to him, a lady—albeit a mid-dle-class lady. For once, though, I wanted to be just a body. I did not want to think, neither about the present nor about the future, and espe-cially not about songs, even sung by Harry Belafonte.

Making love with someone your own size, I was discovering, offered a special thrill that made up for the downside, if you thought being with a man who was short was a drawback, which I have to confess that I did. The symmetry made for a good fit, a match that seemed to eliminate a sense of domination, or maybe the need to find the fit in the first place.

Whatever the explanation, if I needed one, there was something between us that day that resembled the workings of a delicate watch: steady intricate movements, the quiet rhythm of things enmeshed. We found an unexpected kind of peace on the rue Saint-Denis, almost an indifference to our own pleasure. Just to be inside the room represented a respite from struggle, the struggle to be together. Inside the room, the effort was behind us: it was stolen time and time out of time, too.

Irish Coffee

THE AFFAIR WITH HANS HAD put something in motion, but I had no idea where it was going or what the consequences would be. I didn't know what to do—beyond the practical step of going back on the pill, secretly. The more obsessed I became with Hans, the more I withdrew from Jim in my mind, the more he wanted to have sex with me. And I couldn't refuse without getting questions I didn't want to answer. I was trying to get pregnant, wasn't I? We had to have sex for that, didn't we? I was having sex morning, noon, and night. Writing home in December, dropped in among the usual reports of the social whirl and the household developments, I reported my decision to continue the fertility tests with Dr. Hirsch: "It's not that I'm dying to have a kid—far from it at this point—but I'd like to think that everything is all right." My period was two weeks late. I tried all the old wives' remedies I had ever heard about: boiling myself lobster red in the tub and jumping off the bed. I would stare in the mirror to see if I looked different—some people said you could tell by the eyes—and endlessly counted backward and forward on my fingers like Jean Seberg's Patricia in that scene in *Breathless* when she coolly tells Belmondo that she might be pregnant. But unlike Patricia, I was hoping to figure out that it was impossible. What if Jim was sterile, as he thought he might be, and the father of the baby was Hans?

One night, when we were sitting in the living room having Irish coffee, I told Jim I was thinking about having an abortion if I turned out to be pregnant.

"But why?" The space between his eyebrows took on the deep grooves that meant he couldn't bear his own thoughts. It was actually an expression that I loved, the other side of his shouting, the sensitive-man face. The flow of the Irish whisky, warmed by the coffee and sweetened by the thick heavy cream floating at the top of the glass, added to my sense of confusion. Nothing made sense anymore. Didn't I enjoy sitting here with my husband, drinking Irish coffee made by him, looking at our books that had started overflowing the shelves? Why couldn't this be enough? Or the beginning of enough?

I made an appointment to see Dr. Hirsch. I needed to tell him that my period was late and that I wanted to go back on the pill if I wasn't pregnant. He didn't understand why I would start back on the pill now, when I was trying to find out why I hadn't gotten pregnant after eight months of trying. Part of what I told him was the truth, or at least, what I had told Jim—and my parents. The doctor convinced me to do one more fertility test before deciding. He had some questions about my hormonal balance. In the meantime, I left with a sheaf of prescriptions: a urinalysis, an endometrial biopsy, and a new prescription for the *pillule*. I desperately wanted to know what was wrong. Maybe the Tunisian abortion had done me irreparable harm. It would be better to know. It might also be better to be pregnant. Fate would decide. Or my hormones.

After the urine test in a fancy laboratory off the Champs-Élysées, I went home and sat on the bed, waiting by the phone for the lab to call, crumpling the ribs of the corduroy bedspread my mother had made for us. The lab said they would be able to give me the results before dinner. I was supposed to meet Jim on the other side of town for an evening of music with Philippe, who had become fond of Jim and me as stand-ins for my parents, I sometimes thought, now that Philippe and I weren't sleeping together. It was an important dinner because Jim said he had a record company connection, and Philippe wanted to record two of the Schubert impromptus. The phone rang at the end of the afternoon. "I'm sorry to tell you, madame. The results were negative." I made the woman repeat her words. The relief that coursed through my body when I heard the words delivered a clear message about one thing. At that moment, I did not want to be pregnant, even if it also meant that there was something wrong with my body and that I might never have a child.

At the Gare de l'Est, I took the metro to Saint-Germain. It was a direct line, so all I had to do was sit there for thirty minutes, enough time to come down from my high. I began to wonder if I had ever really wanted a child, or if I had just been trying to copy my friends, be like everyone else: you get married; you have a child. End of story. Seberg's character seemed quite unshaken by the possibility of being pregnant and not being sure who the father was. Maybe she'd write a best-selling novel about a girl—Patricia Franchini—who comes to Paris, falls in love with a gangster, gets pregnant, denounces him to the police, and becomes a famous novelist. But this wasn't a movie.

By the time I arrived at Philippe and Anne's apartment I had a violent headache. Philippe pulled me into his office and gave me a codeine pill. "Take another one when you get home, if the pain continues," he said, pressing an almost-full bottle into my hand. He looked inquiringly into my eyes and stroked my hair. The situation that had caused my headache was the sort of thing he would have understood, but I was not in the mood for confiding. When we left, Philippe offered us aluminum Venetian blinds Anne didn't care for that he had received as a gift from a patient. Jim accepted them for the new apartment, making all the predictable puns about jealousy and *jalousie*—the word for blinds in French. "We'll see you back here at the *réveillon*," Philippe said, kissing me on both cheeks and shaking Jim's hand. "New Year's is very soon."

My Grandfather's Watch

I TOLD HANS THAT WE would have to be very careful for a while, even though the immediate danger had passed. "Whatever you want," he would say, with that "I'm just a worker" detachment of his, but I didn't want him to feel discarded now that the boss's wife had had her fun. Talking was impossible at the ranch (even Hans called it "the ranch," and with everybody in jeans and speaking English, it sometimes felt like a small-scale urban version of one). I wanted him to know how confused I was about everything. I wanted to feel him close to me when I explained that I was hoping to go back to New York over Easter vacation. I didn't know what would happen after that.

One day in late March, an old girlfriend of Hans loaned us her studio, near the Place Saint-Michel. We met there in the early afternoon. The small space was tucked under the eaves, with dark exposed beams that Hans had refinished. The windows of the studio looked out over the crowded square. We lay down on the bed, staying on top of the covers.

I had missed his touch and longed for him to caress me. Instead, we just held each other for a while without talking, listening to the traffic. The buses sighed and groaned on the boulevard below, pausing before crossing the Seine. We pressed our bodies tight against each other until we were breathing with a single breath. It seemed perverse not to make love now that we were alone, but I was afraid that if we started, I wouldn't be able to stop.

"So, little fish," Hans said, "maybe you won't come back; maybe you'll bring me to America?"

I was startled by his seamless leap into a new narrative. I wondered whether Hans had contemplated this possibility before I had. It wouldn't have been the first time that romance was entangled with immigration.

As we left the building, Jim suddenly emerged from a doorway across the boulevard. He had followed us to the apartment, he said, and had been waiting for us to come out. He looked like the statue of the Commendatore in *Don Giovanni* who appears onstage in the finale like a god out of a machine. Exuding repressed operatic rage, Jim pulled out the pocket watch that belonged to my grandfather and looked at it theatrically.

"You were up there for two hours and fourteen minutes."

"We were talking."

Jim paused briefly as if considering with an open mind the plausibility of our having spent two hours talking. He always did a very good imitation of being reasonable. But he slipped the watch back into his vest and forced us to go back upstairs. When we got to the apartment, Hans opened the door with his key. Jim looked around, counting the cigarette butts in the ashtray and sniffing for my perfume. He motioned us to walk in ahead of him like guilty children being returned to the scene of the crime. He pulled back the covers on the rumpled bed, and inspected the sheets, which were doubtful, as the French say about linen that is not entirely pristine. It didn't seem to occur to Jim, as I pointed out, that he might have been looking at the sheets that belonged to the owner.

After a while, Jim apologized to Hans, shook hands with him man-to-man, and asked him to leave. Hans hesitated, but Jim waved him off.

When he heard the door close behind Hans, Jim opened his belt and lowered his pants. "If you didn't fuck Hans, fuck me now." When the pounding was over, we left the apartment quickly without changing the sheets. Once outside, I climbed back on the motor scooter in silence; to say anything would have been to acknowledge what had happened between us.

This was not a story I could tell my parents, of course, or even my girlfriends, but I wrote about it to Jonathan Alterman, who had assumed an avuncular role in my life, and who enjoyed long typewritten letters. I couldn't figure out what I was doing, I said, but I couldn't stop doing it. I wasn't in love with Hans, but I couldn't continue with Jim, either. We were sinking huge amounts of money—not even ours—into renovating an apartment, but we couldn't talk to each other without blowing up. France was hard on foreigners. It was exhausting to spend your life in translation. Maybe we'd be better off looking for work in the States, but Jim had made it clear that the only thing he had going for him was being an American in France.

It was the sex; it wasn't the sex. Maybe you couldn't expect marital sex to be a turn-on. I wanted to have a child with Jim and take the next step toward settling down. I didn't want to have a child. I couldn't try to get pregnant if I wasn't sure whose baby it would be.

Jonathan had returned to live in the States. His own life was a mess, he admitted when he wrote back. He was involved with two women and couldn't make up his mind which one to marry. But as usual, he had advice for me. "A psychiatrist would say," he wrote, "that you were telling Jim something by letting yourself get caught; being caught is irrelevant to the reasons you've given me for having a lover. But I'm not a psychiatrist." No, he wasn't a psychiatrist, even though he enjoyed analyzing my situation, but he thought I should make a trip to New York and see one. He had a name for me whenever I was ready.

Why Is It So Hard to Be Happy?

AFTER MONTHS OF BRAGGING TO my parents about my wonderful life in Paris, I announced that I had decided to spend spring vacation in New York. It would mean missing my second wedding anniversary, but I had to take advantage of the dates. "I'm kind of tired, I think," I wrote home. In Paris everything slowed down during Easter. "I need a change of scene," I added, without explaining why. I suspected that Hans was the symptom, not the cause, of my exhaustion, but I was not sure what disease I was suffering from, nor would I ever broach this with my parents. "I'm so thin," I wrote home giddily, "that my old clothes don't fit, my dresses look like tents."

In a series of frantic letters, Dr. Jim filled my parents in on what he labeled my *crise*, offering his diagnosis and the equivalent of the doctor's long list of prescriptions. I had developed a cleanliness mania, he told them, taking showers all the time; I was exposed to a nasty *courant d'air* from the windows that didn't close properly and now I had a cough, aggravated by my smoking. I was too thin. The renovations were dragging on with no end in sight. The weather, the famous Parisian *grisaille,* was depressing; the sky was permanently gray. We should have taken a winter holiday in the snow. We should have gone to the mountains like everybody else, but the money wasn't available. I needed days of sleeping until noon, rest. Maybe I needed a vacation from him. Above all, I needed to see them.

On the flight to New York, I wrapped myself in a blanket, stretched out across the seats in the middle row, and dozed my way across the Atlantic in a codeine-induced haze. Thanks to Philippe, I had an unlimited supply of drugs.

My parents had renovated their apartment after my sister graduated from college and moved out. The only place for me to sleep was on a small sofa bed in what had become the dining room (it had originally been the bedroom I shared with my sister, before I appropriated the maid's room for myself). Camped out on the sofa bed, my first night back, with no doors separating me from the rest of the apartment, I felt like a guest who had already outstayed her welcome.

It was April in New York, alternately balmy and bitter. In a letter dated the day of our second wedding anniversary, Jim reminded my mother of a conversation they had had in Paris, the summer after we were married. Walking from the Hôtel d'Angleterre, where they were staying, toward our apartment, Jim pointed to the *auto-école* where I had learned to drive.

"Nancy got her *permis* on the second try," he said. "She only missed it the first time because of parallel parking, but she won't take the car out by herself."

"She's your problem now," my mother had said to him then with a cynical laugh. He thought he had solved the problem, he wrote, in the good-son-in-law mode he had adopted with my parents. But two years later he had to recognize how abysmally he failed. He spiraled into a litany of abjection—his ignorance, self-delusion, rigidity.

At dinner, my mother read that part of the letter aloud. I was touched but also baffled by Jim's extravagant show of self-knowledge. And I resented being passed along as a problem.

   I HAD ARRANGED TO MEET Jonathan for lunch at a restaurant near the Museum of Natural History. I had come to feel at ease with him and somewhat detached, even though I couldn't help remembering our scene at the Pont-Royal. Or maybe it was because I remembered the scene so well that I felt safe—beyond nostalgia, beyond temptation. He could be trusted, I thought, despite our history, to consider my case with the perspective of a journalist—unlike my parents. They had always believed my staying on year after year in Paris was a bad idea, and they had always had their doubts about Jim. Now, though, having me back so soon after the marriage could be embarrassing. How were they going to explain this to their family and friends? No one in their family had ever been divorced, and then there was the not inconsiderable amount of money they had invested in the apartment only six months earlier. In some ways, having me off their hands and in Jim's—however inadequate a provider he might have turned out to be—had its advantages. Replying, when asked, that I was married and living in Paris carried a certain cachet, especially compared to my sister Andrea, whose East Village address could not be mentioned.

Jonathan ordered Gibsons for both of us.

"You sounded desperate in your letters," he said, taking my hand across the table and raising it to his lips, a European gesture he managed to pull off without looking affected.

"I want to go back to Paris, but I can't imagine going back to Jim." That was the first time I had put my dilemma so succinctly. It was a kind of relief.

After reading the wedding announcement in the *Times,* Jonathan had sent me a note saying, "How nice that someone I remember fondly has found what she wants." I remembered feeling surprised by the formulation then; it was painful to think about now, and even harder to explain. How had I lost so quickly what I passionately wanted only two years earlier? That was the crux of my misery, and that's what Jonathan was after.

We both ordered hamburgers and another round of drinks. I knew I would regret the second Gibson. I was almost starting to regret the lunch. There was something about Jonathan—Jewish men?—that never failed to irritate me, even though I was drawn to his intelligence. The way, I was thinking as I watched him take in my story, Jewish men seem to think they have your number—if you're a Jewish woman— and that it's their tribal obligation to bring it to your attention. David was the master of the move. Mark did too, even though we were only collaborating on a book. It was somewhat different with Jim, who was no less eager to prove that he knew more than I did in all areas. I sensed how important what he knew was to him, whereas intellectual condescension just rolled off his precursors in the genre like a little wave of entitlement. Still, I had no regrets about not having given Jonathan another chance when he came through Paris again and wanted to rewind the reel. "See what you're missing," he seemed to be saying with every question. I did. But I had not forgotten what happened in bed—and afterward.

I HAD SCRIBBLED A LINE from *Darling* in my diary. It was the scene when Julie Christie says to Dirk Bogarde as they look out over the Thames, "Why is it so hard to be happy?" Maybe it wasn't about Jim. Maybe I just didn't know how to be happy.

"I thought being married would make me happy. I guess I don't like being married as much as I thought I would."

"Nobody does."

Hundreds of people were streaming past the plateglass window at the restaurant where we were seated, heading for a demonstration against the Vietnam War in Central Park. We could hear the crowds chanting, "Hey, hey, LBJ, how many kids did you kill today?" Why weren't we outside joining the march instead of drinking Gibsons and talking about marriage? Everyone looked incredibly young. I felt old, too old to march. Besides, it was drizzling.

"You had an affair to create a crisis," Jonathan said, after a while, as we watched the kids walking by.

"That doesn't make sense. We had this incredible apartment. Things were starting to happen."

"Ask a psychiatrist."

We were back to that. Jonathan was the first person I had ever known who had seen a psychiatrist. My parents always ridiculed psychiatry. Some of their favorite jokes were about people they knew—friends, though they would never tell us which ones—who had spent years and money in analysis only to emerge utterly unchanged but complacent. They did the same destructive things they had always done but didn't feel bad about it anymore. My mother played tennis with a psychiatrist and thought he was the most neurotic man she knew—also a very sore loser. I was dubious about going to see a psychiatrist myself, but I decided to make an appointment with Dr. Mendelsohn, Jonathan's doctor. I had nothing to lose, and Jonathan claimed it had helped him figure out what he wanted to do: get divorced.

You Don't Love Your Husband

DR. AARON MENDELSOHN HAD AN office on Central Park West. He sat behind his desk during the consultation, asking questions (sounding exactly like Jonathan) and listening sternly as I described my situation. I tried to be as entertaining as possible, which was always what I did when I visited doctors, but he was not amused.

"I don't know what to do."

Dr. Mendelsohn nodded indifferently.

I rattled on from there, telling the doctor about my previous boyfriends, gathering speed toward the denouement, as I described the narrative arc of the present disaster, from the money borrowed from my parents, to the renovation and the school and our hopes for its future, and then to the affair with Hans. Picking someone like Hans—someone completely impossible as a replacement, even as a lover—was crazy, I concluded.

You probably weren't supposed to say you were "crazy" to a psychiatrist. That was his job. I stopped talking and waited for his response.

"You don't love your husband."

"How can you know that?" How could he know at the end of an hour what I had spent months analyzing in infinite detail?

"You don't *sound* like someone who loves her husband."

"What does that mean?"

"It means," he said, looking at me wearily as if he had heard it all before (which he no doubt had), "that if you loved your husband you wouldn't be here."

I stared back at him. Wasn't this circular? Or if not circular, facile? What kind of logic was that? Had he never heard of ambivalence? The more I looked at him, the more I realized that he not only sounded like Jonathan (or vice versa) but looked like Jonathan. Another middle-aged (though he must have been older than Jonathan), overweight, smug, Jewish guy whose mother had probably loved him too much—as long as we were throwing clichés around.

What was I supposed to do?

"Stay here, live with your parents, and see me intensively—at least three times a week."

His prescription was so arbitrary that I regained confidence in my own judgment.

"I'm working on a book with a collaborator. We signed a contract."

Dr. Mendelsohn was unimpressed. "You can finish the book by mail."

Nothing mattered except for psychoanalysis. How could he be so sure, when I wasn't? It felt as if he were already losing interest in my case.

"Think about it," he added abruptly, "and come back at the end of the week. I have an opening Friday afternoon." I wanted to say no, but I thought about how the psychiatrist in *Suddenly Last Summer* vindicates the rebellious girl. Maybe he would rescue me. Too bad he didn't look like Montgomery Clift.

Friday he recapped my history. I wanted to marry David. My parents disapproved, and then suddenly I had to get away from him. I went to France. Then I wanted to marry Bernard. And as soon as my parents gave me a chance to bail out, I did. All they had to do was ask.

He paused long enough for me to guess what was coming. I knew my story too.

I take the leap and marry Jim. To my surprise, my parents go along with it after the fact. And just as it looks as though this wasn't the worst possible choice I could have made, I destroy the situation by having an affair with another, even more unsuitable man. I created the crisis because I couldn't handle their approval. It was all part of the same pattern. Could I see that?

The doctor looked at me with a flicker of self-satisfaction. I recognized a variant of Jonathan's analysis: creating a crisis. I asked if he had ever heard of structuralism, of Roland Barthes. Wasn't that the same thing, looking at the structure of the stories instead of getting caught up in the details? Seeing the pattern of the narrative, whatever the content. I decided that was not the kind of answer he had in mind. He didn't seem very impressed by anything to do with French ideas.

He went on, retelling my past according to his theory. It wasn't about the men; it was about the men in relation to my parents. I hadn't learned how to separate. I get as far away from my parents as I can by choosing unsuitable men. To break their hold over me, I have sex with my parents' friends. But that doesn't work either. So I try to make my life resemble theirs, turn Jim into my father, pretend I'm a housewife like my mother, model my home on theirs. When that fails, I turn against my own choice and return home. First the good daughter, then the bad daughter. Whatever the story, I'm a daughter, not an independent person.

As the doctor was talking, I could feel a *crise* coming on. It was embarrassing to have someone you didn't know seem to know all about you. On the other hand, I couldn't see my way forward. Was going backward the right direction? When I returned to his office later that week, I was still skeptical.

Was this what psychiatrists did? Make you feel ashamed and

stupid? I had everything backward. Cause was merely effect. I didn't
want to get pregnant because I wanted to remain a child, my parents'
and Jim's. I had an affair to avoid getting pregnant. That had a weird
kind of logic, assuming, of course, that what I thought I wanted was
the opposite of what I *really* wanted. In my unconscious, if I believed
in the unconscious. Did I? The last thing I wanted to hear about was
about my relationship to my parents. I could see the part about the
pattern of repetition. I just couldn't imagine his solution to the current
crisis: sitting in his office—not to mention lying on the couch—three
times a week while living at home. But my time was up again; the
doctor was already ushering me out. Clearly, I wasn't serious about
solving my problems or I'd be doing exactly what he advised, signing
on for analysis with him.

Despite her long-standing disdain for psychiatry, my mother
was enthusiastic about Dr. Mendelsohn's recommendation that I
return home.

"You don't love your husband," the doctor had said at the first
session.

Maybe I didn't love my husband. Maybe I didn't want a husband.
It was hard to know. I knew I wasn't happy, but was being unhappy the
same thing as not loving someone? How could you tell?

While I was in Manhattan, my husband was writing to my parents
twice daily, in addition to writing to me. He dated our crisis from taking
over the new apartment. I wrote back to Jim and said I wouldn't decide
anything until I returned to Paris. I wanted to believe what he said in his
letters. That he wanted to try.

I almost didn't recognize Jim from the sweet and compromising
tone of his letters. How would our life be better? We'd take more vaca-
tions. We had stopped traveling after we married. He would be more
organized about finances (not that I had any idea of how much money we
did or didn't have). He would pay me for the classes I taught. He would
encourage me to get a doctorate (and have Hans make finishing the study
and the shower a priority). He would not yell at the workers. He would be

nicer to my friends. In a word (many words, as always, once he put pen to paper), he would be a changed man, the man he wanted to be, the man I thought I had married.

In his reply to Jim's letters, my father noted his son-in-law's failure to send me money in New York on our anniversary and expressed his expectation that Jim would adopt a "responsible and sensible approach," whatever our future turned out to be.

My Father Plays Detective

BEFORE I RETURNED TO PARIS, my father revealed that he had started doing research on Jim. We were sitting in the kitchen having coffee after dinner.

"Why didn't you ask me what you wanted to know?"

"Because you believe everything he tells you. And obviously the guy is incapable of a straight answer."

My father loved straight answers.

"And then there was all the shilly-shallying to get us the details about his diplomas for the wedding announcement in the *Times*."

"I told you we didn't want an announcement."

"Why not? If you weren't hiding something." For years my parents had been convinced I was hiding something from them. Of course I was. Do you voluntarily offer information to the FBI?

Finally, my father dropped his bomb. "Jim doesn't have a BA," he said, as if he had discovered that Jim had served time in prison. "He never graduated from college. I'm sure all the other diplomas he says he has are completely fabricated."

While my father left the kitchen to get his briefcase, I sat at the table torn between incredulity and relief. I didn't think Jim was hiding anything behind his beard (my mother's theory) besides a weak chin, but I knew—without knowing—that he was consumed by secrets. If I hadn't found the letter in his pocket, would I ever have known he wasn't really divorced yet? Maybe he had been married to someone else before her. Where did he go on Sunday afternoons? What happened to the money that came in for ELF? Was he or wasn't he an alcoholic? I should have known Jim could lie about anything, given the way he charmed potential clients about the school's future (I guess the school was real enough in his head). I tried to figure out whether I cared, whether the missing degree mattered.

Putting the reply from the Registrar's Office on the table, a document that he had obtained by posing as a future employer, my father asked, "If he could lie about something as basic as a college degree, what else do you think he has lied to us about?"

Everything made a new kind of sense. Jim's pedantry was the show-off knowledge of an autodidact. All the reading and the ravenous consumption of facts were the flip side of the lie. He had built an entire identity in Europe from the missing diploma. He must have smooth-talked some bureaucrat into giving him a French degree equivalent to the fictitious American BA and then kept trading one credential for another, the degrees from Madrid and Perugia my parents included in the wedding announcement. Jim couldn't speak Spanish. I almost admired the fraud. It was like a Patricia Highsmith novel—minus the murder. No wonder Jim said he could never make it in the States.

"It might be grounds for annulment," my father concluded, pleased with the idea.

"We're not talking about divorce yet."

I wanted to see Jim again, away from the harsh realities of New York, in the gray zone of our life together in Paris.

The Confession

"GOOD FLIGHT, SANE RECEPTION. JIM met me at Orly wearing his black suit and carrying red roses," I wrote as soon as I returned to Paris. "He's lost weight and looks good. Jim is being reasonable—for him."

On the drive from the airport, as we threaded through traffic in the little green car we had fallen in love with on the honeymoon and that now had begun to fail part by part, I told Jim I wanted us to have separate rooms for a while. He nodded. When we got to the apartment, I put my bags in the little back room.

"I want you to sleep in the bedroom. I promise I won't wake you."

"That's a promise you can't keep."

I was too tired to insist. What difference could one more time possibly make? Jim woke me at five.

"Just this once." I closed my eyes and waited for him to finish.

Later that morning I suggested we go downstairs to the café across the street to discuss the situation over coffee. I thought Jim would control himself in a public space, especially in the local café where he had a reputation to maintain—the counter at which he had his morning coffee and late night cognac. If nothing else, Jim believed in appearances. The American professor and his charming wife.

We chose a table in the back, away from the crowd of men standing at the counter. Jim beckoned to the waiter and, as if nothing had changed, ordered for both of us. "Un thé pour madame, et une tartine beurrée." Just an espresso for him and a glass of water—the water to show me he was serious about losing weight. The waiter didn't understand English, but we waited for him to leave before speaking.

"I know you're having an affair with Hans."

"I'm not discussing Hans. I want to talk about how we can get through the next few months with as little damage as possible." Was Dr. Mendelsohn right that I didn't love Jim? Looking at him across the table, at the soft creases around his eyes, I could see that he was suffering. I felt compassion for him, but I also felt the same kind of certainty I had when breaking up with David. I just could not go on.

"So you're leaving?"

"I guess so. I interviewed for a teaching job in a high school. I hope I don't get it. But whatever happens, I'm not going back until August. I have to finish the book."

"When did it start with Hans?"

"Please stop obsessing about Hans. He's not the problem. You are."

"How can I be the problem? I still love you."

"It's not about love." I paused before asking my father's question. He had harped on Jim's financial failures. "Is there enough money to finish the renovations?"

Jim shrugged and looked sullen. "What difference does it make?" We had spent hours in this café since getting the apartment. It was exactly the kind of place Jim loved. The list of wines was inscribed in chalk on a blackboard above the counter, along with the sandwiches—the *rillettes* and *saucisson sec* Jim considered authentic enough to eat. While the waiter unloaded the breakfast tray, I prepared to tell Jim about my father's research, as he called it. I knew that whatever bonds of love remained would be broken beyond repair when I did.

But to assuage my guilt about Hans, I needed to put Jim in the wrong. I lit a cigarette.

"I know about the BA. My father wrote to the registrar."

Jim said nothing. His hooded eyes filled with rage. I would pay for this. I just didn't know how or when.

He went back to his line of questioning about Hans, exactly as though I had not exposed the fabulation.

"When did it start?"

"Hans is not the point. Even you know that."

"I agree. Hans is going back to Germany next month with Ingrid. They're having problems with their papers. He won't be working for us much longer." I experienced a strange sense of relief.

"Tell me, please," he continued, "tell me, I just need to know. After that, it won't matter," he said, taking my hand in his.

I had been over this with Jonathan. I had been over this with Leo. Both of them had lectured me: no matter what he says, don't admit anything. I knew they were right, especially considering how volatile Jim could be, but they were men, and besides there was some part of me that *wanted* to tell, to get it over with. That must be how they get criminals to confess, I thought, when there's no real evidence. After a while, you just can't stand the questions; you tell the truth out of despair or boredom.

All I had to do was say no. But I said yes. I said yes, thinking that I was going to leave anyway, that maybe he would stop obsessing if he knew. Maybe it would make it easier for us in the end. Maybe I owed him the truth. Maybe I wanted to hurt him for how things had turned out—for messing up the ranch. I didn't need a session with a psychiatrist to know that I preferred to blame other people for my mistakes.

The minute the word came out of my mouth, I knew I had made the wrong choice. Jim's face reddened with rage. He threw some change on the table and motioned with his head in the direction of the staircase that led to the apartment.

As we climbed the four flights of stairs, I tried to read the expression of his back. I could tell that he was weary. I could also tell that nothing would stop him from enacting his anger. I wished I had turned around and gone back to the café, gone to stay with Monique and Alain, but I kept following him, the way a kid dumbly submits to paternal punishment—even fetches the strap hanging in the closet—awaiting her doom, convinced that it is as inevitable as unjust. We walked down the long hallway, where I had spent intense hours scraping the layers of wallpaper and where the exposed beams that extended floor to ceiling now almost glowed between the rough, white surfaces. We turned right into the living area, where the parquet had been repaired, and into the kitchen. I hadn't realized how much had been accomplished while I was in New York. That part of what Jim had told my father was true. The place was coming together. I looked around the kitchen, at the rustic table that fit so much better here than it did in the previous apartments. Why was I giving this up? Wasn't this my space too? Why was I leaving it all to Jim, who would still be living in his cold-water flat in Montparnasse if it weren't for me?

With a faint smile, Jim showed me the detail of the cabinets—how cleverly Hans had attached them to the supporting beams. I remembered Hans standing on the ladder, trying to get the doors to hang properly. Suddenly, silently, Jim tossed out everything the cabinets contained: the grains tumbled onto the floor; rice hit the windowpanes; cans and bottles rolled across the floor, scattering wildly. Then he carefully removed the Majolica collection from the shelves and, picking up a crowbar, pulled the cabinets down from the walls. I stood there, frozen in witness, while he dismantled what had been the center of our life. Finally, Jim walked out of the kitchen into the sitting room and tried to pry up the floorboards that Hans had so carefully fitted together. When the boards resisted, he started cursing, flailing, kicking whatever stood in his way. I could tell that he wanted to kick me, too. Instead he pushed me ahead of him into the bedroom. It was almost as though we both remembered at the same time the scene in the borrowed apartment at the Place Saint-Michel. He threw me down on the mattress.

Notre Dame

Despite what Jim had said, Hans was still working on the apartment. A few days after the scene in the café, we received a cheerful postcard from Tangier, where he and Ingrid had gone for vacation. Hans rehung the cabinets and repaired the damage to the floor when he returned, without asking for an explanation. I knew from Leo that Hans was afraid of Jim, but he needed the job. Even I continued teaching classes when Jim insisted. That's how it was.

One Friday evening, when Hans was finishing up, Jim announced that the three of us were going out to dinner—he was feeling affluent, he said, with new clients on the horizon. We drove to a restaurant not far from the apartment. Over couscous Jim and Hans talked about the renovation, what still had to be completed: the new toilet in the front entrance, the lighting throughout the apartment, the carpeting in the classroom spaces. The meal dragged on as Jim piled merguez sausages and vegetables onto his plate and finished a second bottle of Algerian wine. I pressed Hans's foot under the table.

After dinner, Jim announced that we would accompany Hans home. On the Île Saint-Louis, Jim abruptly stopped the car as though he had just thought of something. He said he wanted to smoke his cigar while looking at the back of Notre-Dame, his favorite view in Paris. When he climbed out of the Austin, Jim turned his head and told Hans to bring his toolbox. As the three of us walked toward the Pont de la Tournelle, the bridge connecting the island to the Left Bank, I saw in a flash what Jim had in mind. I knew his passion for puns. We stopped at the river's edge. Jim took the toolbox, opened the latch and, one by one, dropped Hans's precious tools into the dark currents of the Seine below, beginning with the screwdriver.

It was like a one-act play, a pantomime in which none of us had speaking parts. Director and actor, Jim had cast Hans as Abelard, the intruder into the house who is castrated for seducing the master's daughter; never mind that I was his wife, not his daughter. The little scene had required only a few minutes to unfold. Hans missed the reference but got the point. Jim relit his cigar, appearing satisfied with the performance. After a while, he said he would walk home and told me to drop Hans off at his hotel. In an almost friendly voice he suggested that Hans take a couple of days off from work, get some rest. "You look tired," he said. Hans nodded.

I still hadn't figured out how to turn the car lights on or put the Austin into reverse, but I delivered Hans to his hotel in Montparnasse, steering in the dark. We sat in the car across the street from the hotel entrance, cut off from each other and lonely in the aftermath of our humiliation.

Overdose

EARLY THE NEXT MORNING, JIM drove to Sancerre to replenish our stock of wine. He woke me to find out where I had left the car. I had pulled in straight in front of the police station on the little square opposite our building, jubilant at having escaped the trial of parallel parking.

I was completely alone for the first time in more than a year. It was a Saturday, and the workers would not be coming in. I made a pot of tea and took it to the back room. I sat on the edge of my bed for a while, drinking the tea and smoking. I could still feel Hans's presence in the room, his hands on my jeans. The intensity of the eastern light outside the courtyard window meant that spring had finally come to Paris. It wasn't a warm, sunny New York spring but the bright, chilly May weather that makes French people run outside with their coats open and turn their faces hungrily to the sun. "There is little I can tell you about the emotional scene," I had written home after the long Easter break. "Jim has been trying hard, but the old frictions are still there—neither of us can change that. I have no doubts about my plans to separate from him. The only thing that makes me a little sad is the idea of leaving Paris—it's so beautiful now—cabs are cheap and cafés everywhere—and one feels safe."

I thought about how much I wanted to sleep, how little I wanted to deal with Jim, even Hans. I thought of the work on the book that had to be done with Mark, packing up, sending things back to New York: leaving. Did I fit Dr. Mendelsohn's portrait of me: a girl doomed to repetition? How exactly was I supposed to change that? The tape of our last session kept playing in my head. Do you see a pattern here? I took a Valium with my tea, hoping to tune out the voices. You don't love your husband. I swallowed another Valium. I was starting to feel drowsy. When was Jim coming back? Probably the next day. Maybe he hadn't told me. It didn't matter. I started inserting the suppositories Dr. Finkelstein had prescribed for my cramps; this was a use of the medication unforeseen by the drug manufacturers. Then I popped a few more little yellow pills, alternating with the codeine Philippe had given me—just in case. I fell back on the bed. As I began to feel the muscle relaxants finally moving through my bloodstream, weighing down my limbs, I reached for the half-empty Jameson bottle that I had taken from Jim's bedside table. That would push me over the edge of consciousness, I was sure. I propped myself up on one elbow and managed a few sips.

JIM WAS STANDING ON THE threshold of the little room. I thought I could make out Mark standing behind him. Mark had insisted on seeing for himself when for two days in a row Jim had told him on the phone that I was sleeping.

"She appears to be alive," Jim said to Mark with the wintry smile he had begun to adopt when referring to me.

"How long has she been lying there like this?"

"I have no idea," Jim answered, looking bored. "She's not my problem anymore."

When Mark realized that I couldn't sit up by myself, he called

SOS Médecins. I heard him explaining the situation over the phone. "Overdose" was one of those fetish words that had entered the discourse via *franglais*.

"Stand up, please, madame," the young doctor said. I hadn't moved for two days. Mark pulled me to my feet. "Can you stand by yourself? If not, you will have to have your stomach pumped. Suicide is against the law in this country, you know. You could have killed yourself," he added, in case I had missed the point.

I tottered briefly and fell back on the bed. Why wouldn't they all go away and let me sleep?

"You are the husband?" the doctor asked Mark, practicing his English, and disconcerted by Jim's indifference. Mark said yes—no point trying to explain Jim. The doctor told him to take me to the *cabinet* to see whether I could urinate. When we returned, the doctor was examining the remains of the suppository wrappers and bottles that had contained the medication. He shook his head. Addressing Mark, and ignoring me as if I were an annoyance he couldn't wait to erase from his busy schedule, the doctor explained that I should be encouraged to eat, exercise, and spend some time in the sun.

The overdose had been my last idea. It wasn't exactly an idea, of course, more like a surrender to the sense of failure I had been trying to ward off all that year. The marriage plot had collapsed, as had the quest for freedom that had brought me to Paris in the first place. I had come to the end of a road, the path that had taken me to the city of my dreams.

I was immobilized by disappointment.

For a few days in May, I walked with Mark, leaning on his arm like an old lady, through the arcades of the Palais-Royal where Colette spent the last years of her life, writing and being cared for by her third and much younger husband. As we made our way slowly around the square, Mark talked to me about the future—his intellectual ambitions. I marveled at his sense of entitlement, at his conviction that the world was there for the taking.

His anticipation was matched only by my dread.

"Why don't you come with me to the south of France?" Mark

proposed one afternoon. A friend had offered him the use of a house. In the 1950s, when property in France was still cheap, Anthony had come into a small inheritance and acquired a farmhouse high up in the hills behind Saint-Tropez. For a considerable sum a neighbor rented part of the land for his vineyard. A one-room shack came with the property and Anthony invited friends to stay there when he was in the mood for company.

"The doctor said you should spend some time in the sun," Mark pressed me. "We can make some progress on the book," he continued patiently, as though speaking to a slow child.

"I don't know. What's the point?"

But the second time Mark asked, I said yes. When I told Dominique, a senior professor and Couderc's colleague, what we were planning, she looked at me skeptically. She was friendly with Mark and had known me since my days at Middlebury summer school.

"Another man? Already?"

"But he's like a brother," I said, "and we're going to work."

I sometimes thought Mark could have been my brother. We had the same kinky hair and long, oval faces. One of the uncles on my mother's side, the one who had made money in the coffee and tea business, was called Rothberg. The name gave our physical resemblance a resonance it might otherwise have lacked. Besides, the fact that Mark had braved Jim's hostility made me want to trust him enough to embark on three weeks of tête-à-tête in the country.

"Ma chère," Dominique said, unpersuaded, "you've just left your father; don't start with your brother."

The idea of a literary partnership appealed to me. Maybe I was starting something. I hoped it wasn't about sex. I prepared a little suitcase I kept under the bed in the back room, ready for my escape. In early June I met Mark at the Gare de Lyon. The skies were still gray in Paris and we shivered on the platform waiting for the train south.

Three Weeks in Provence

THE FARMHOUSE LOOKED OUT OVER sloping terraces and the vineyard below. A shortcut—a narrow winding path made up of rough white pebbles—connected the main building to the guest quarters, where Mark and I had set up shop. The road sign for the hamlet seemed to point toward an abandoned dovecote, a perfectly round tower of stones with a tiny window at the top. The shack, as Anthony referred to it, was actually a small stone building tucked away behind the dovecote and set deep into the side of the hill, with a long flight of rough-hewn steps leading down to the entrance. The room had a primitive fireplace and a sleeping loft. In early June it was hot during the day, but at night it was cold enough to need a fire.

Mornings, we worked at the long harvest table under the sleeping loft. Later, we baked in the sun, reading novels or writing letters, the radio tuned to France-Musique. We were happy to be far from the crowds of tourists already flocking to the Riviera, with our serious books and the local herbs with which I lavishly perfumed our *omelettes aux fines herbes:* thyme, sage, and rosemary that grew wild. The rosemary reached the size of small bushes. It was the land of the *bouquet garni.* In the early evening, Mark would walk our letters over to the big house, leaving them for the postman and picking up our mail after a chat with Anthony. On his way back, Mark would stop and buy fresh eggs from one of the neighbors, an old woman who kept a few chickens in her backyard along with a friendly goat. Every few days Anthony drove us to local markets, where we stocked up on cheese, bread, and olives.

The rituals of our daily life in the little stone house reminded me strangely of the honeymoon weeks in Ireland. The landscape was less green in Provence, of course, and there were no vineyards or olive groves in Connemara, but the narrow pathways, the proximity of the sea, and the isolation all brought images of that pastoral interval back to me. The geography was the least of it, I suppose. Hidden away from the world with another man whose supreme values were books and food, I relived the endless summer hours in Ireland with Jim reading and listening to Radio Caroline—when the ranch was still the dream.

After the violent episodes in Paris, I had been afraid to let Jim know how to reach me, but in one of those hopeful gestures that experience should have taught me to resist, in the end I gave him my address. I didn't think he would hunt me down in the *maquis.* Jim wrote almost daily, as if we were merely separated by distance. What was I reading and thinking? my husband wanted to know. Jim had spent time in the south of France before he met me, and his letters included recommendations for the best *tomates provençales,* the best coffee—complete with hand-drawn maps and arrows pointing directions to a newsstand in Sainte-Maxime where you could buy the daily *Herald Tribune.* If we had no future together, the past impinged almost daily on the present, the endlessly proliferating details of our separation: the car that he wanted to unload, classes for me to teach when I got back to Paris, plans for selling the school now that I was leaving. He promised to send money as soon as he made some.

Instead of a check, I received a series of black-and-white photographs of me taken during the honeymoon. In the first one, the Austin is parked along the side of the road and I'm posing on top of a picnic table, leaning back on my elbows in classic girly calendar mode, with my back slightly arched. I'm looking back over my shoulder at the camera with a mocking smile as if to say, "I know this is ridiculous." Jim had cropped the photograph of his pinup wife wearing her new push-up bra and mailed it in the form of a postcard: on the back, a message demanding my recipe for barley pilaf.

The next day, a second photograph arrived in postcard format. I'm looking away from the camera into the far distance, in the pained-heroine mode I thought made me look sultry. Jim pleaded again for the recipe. Two days later, I received a third picture, this time cut up into twelve fragments that he had carefully glued to a piece of 8-by-11-inch cardboard. The pieces of the photograph were slivered like shards of a broken mirror, the trees growing upside down. In the margins between the scraps of my mutilated body in the landscape, Jim had placed the letters spelling "barley" in English and "*orge*" in French. The photograph was accompanied by a mock-heroic history of the grain, "Notes toward a Definition of Barley."

Mark thought the cut-ups looked like the work of a psycho.

"He's playing detective with the photographs," I explained. "Like the guy in *Blow-Up*, looking for clues to an unsolved crime. He's trying to get back to the way things were between us when I cooked for him."

"Did you ever wonder why the most important thing about you is your mother's recipe for barley pilaf? But that he begs for it by putting you in a sexy pose?"

"It's a pun. 'Orge' for 'orgy.' Jim's like my parents. He doesn't believe in the unconscious."

Mark couldn't understand why I maintained contact with a man who hadn't cared enough about me to call the doctor when he saw me drifting into a coma.

"He didn't care if you died."

"I didn't either."

The stream of photographs reminded me of the flurry of *pneus* Jim had sent me after the job interview for ELF and the letters he wrote to me while I was in New York during our second anniversary. It was

impossible to have a face-to-face conversation with Jim that got anywhere. Whenever I approached a difficult topic, he would fall silent.
He would blink his eyes slowly, as though a door was closing. On
paper, it was just the opposite. Not that the flow of words brought me
closer to the truth—about the degree, about why he couldn't return to
America, about the money. In his letters to my father, he had sketched
a poignant self-portrait of the dutiful if bereft son-in-law that had
briefly convinced my father that a sane denouement to our drama was
still possible. In the postcards to me, he played the sulky husband
left behind to earn a living while the wife vacationed in the south of
France, as if we were just another bourgeois family—minus the two
children, of course.

Jim kept writing to me—and to my father—because we were still
involved in the story of the marriage, even if the marriage was over. We
were caught up in the rhythms of an epistolary novel, where the characters continue to correspond while saying that they are not going to write
anymore because they have nothing to say. The last word, until the editor
intervenes, is always just another invitation to respond.

"We now have a modus vivendi of sorts," I wrote. "We both have
our 'freedom' but remain friends."

Had we ever been friends?

Leaving Jim the apartment, my lawyer-father believed, was a serious error: "He has the apartment and you are kicking about; he is using
the car and you are using the subway; he has a bank account and you are
without your own funds (not even the equivalent of what his teachers got
but which you did not, as his teacher); he is not living up to his marital
obligation of support. In New York, if he were to tell a Judge that he
had no money to pay he'd be laughed at—you pay—beg or borrow or
go to jail. If you can't get money, at least get your freedom via divorce or
annulment *at his cost*."

As usual, my father had the facts right: I was living out of a suitcase, while Jim had the huge apartment paid for by my parents. Jim had
access to the company bank account, and I was reduced to getting hand-
outs from home. But the indignation felt wrong. Would the hypothetical
Judge make the same decision if he knew about my sidebar with the

carpenter? Would my father? But then, I couldn't tell him about the suicide attempt either.

I was drowning in a sea of stories that would never get told.

Mark admired the rhetorical flourish, antithesis, and chiasmus
with which my father laid out the situation. My father, whom Mark had
started calling Papa K., insisted on connecting the dots, showing me how
to understand life in the "real world," beginning with rule number one,
which he had invoked when I told him belatedly about our deal for the
book: "There is nothing wrong or immoral in looking out for your own
interests." Couderc had continued to be evasive about when we could
expect to be paid. He was waiting, he said, to hear from the publishers
in New York about the American version of the book. Mark thought
Couderc was capable of rejecting the preface to justify not paying us for
the work we had already done; he turned out to be right. Everything I
disliked about my father's approach to me was what Mark longed to see
in a threatening letter to Couderc.

"He should have been *your* father."

Halfway through the stay, Mark and I finished the preface. We
celebrated the end of our collaboration by smoking some of the grass
that Leo had given me to use when he came to see me in Paris after
the overdose. Good stuff, he had promised, very clean. Better than
Valium, baby. I didn't think anything was better than Valium. Mark
rolled the joints with care, making them tight and slim. We were
stretched out on top of the bed on the sleeping loft, passing the joint
between us, thinking of the people we could enlist in making trouble
for Couderc, if he betrayed us. We reviewed the list of senior col-
leagues at the Institute.

Suddenly, Mark leaned over and kissed me, very tentatively, on
the lips.

"Hey."

"What's wrong?"

"I don't think this is a good idea."

"Why not?" Mark said, picking up the roach with tweezers and
taking a last puff of the joint. "We said we'd see what happened."

"That was in the abstract."

"You don't find me attractive," Mark said, with the slightly accusatory tone he adopted whenever I didn't go along with his wishes. It was the other side of his sweetness.

"That's not what I meant." I paused, thinking about Dominique's warning. "You have a great body. I told you that."

"So what's the problem, then?"

"I'm not ready. It's much too soon."

Mark slipped his hand under the miniskirt I had been wearing for our sunbathing sessions.

"Why don't we just see what happens," he said, moving his hand slowly up my thigh. I was stoned enough to lie back down. Maybe Mark was right. Who could say what would happen? This wasn't the worst beginning. He slipped off his shorts and made his way inside me quickly after that, as if he wanted everything to be over as soon as possible.

"What's the matter?" I asked, relieved to have him next to me in the bed and not inside of me.

"I need more encouragement."

"I told you I didn't think I was ready. Besides, you are incredibly wide."

Mark took the size comment as a compliment.

"Do you know what Dominique said when I told her I was coming down here with you?" I asked, lighting a cigarette.

"No, what?"

"That you were homosexual."

"Did she tell you that she was lesbian?"

"She didn't have to. So are you?"

"I prefer the company of women," Mark said, after a pause. "But I'm more attracted to men."

"So you've slept with Anthony, I suppose."

"Everyone sleeps with Anthony."

None of this was supposed to count. After all, we were free. Mark refused to believe that being "more attracted to men" could possibly have played a role in what happened between us in bed. Arguing with Mark was like arguing with Jim when he was feeling wounded—his mind was locked into a position of righteousness to which he had thrown away the key long ago. With Jim, I couldn't help knowing the hurt was there behind the anger. I didn't know Mark well enough to guess the path back to the pain, and he had no intention of going there with me.

Mark had planned an odyssey for himself for the rest of the summer, sailing from Marseille to Istanbul, and then finally moving on to Israel, with maybe a stay in Greece, on his way back to Europa, as he liked to say. He was thinking of going to the island of Seriphos, where friends had offered him a house. I could meet him there for a few days.

We parted at the local train station. Mark was taking a train to Marseille and I was returning to Paris.

"You should go to Greece, even if I don't," he said, frowning as we stood on the platform, waiting for his train. "It will be cheaper than the hotel in Paris."

"Jim needs me to be there. We have business to deal with. The car. It's complicated." I shrugged, knowing I could never make Mark understand why I felt I owed Jim something.

"You enjoy feeling guilty," he said, boarding the train and pleased at having the last word.

The Crash

"I HAD NEVER KNOWN THIS," a woman in one of Colette's novels says of a new lover, "the intelligent joy of the flesh that recognizes its master." I flushed when I read that sentence. On the train back to Paris I copied the lines into my diary. I was still trying to come to terms with the irruption of desire that had fractured my marriage.

> Yesterday in the restaurant—a troubling couple. The woman's face reflected the ardor—the word does apply here—of devouring attentiveness that I know to have been mine. I was fascinated—wanting to look—and disturbed by what I saw. I recognized the basic and animal-like quality of her attachment—it was mine—it still haunts me—and were I to see H. again—it still would be there, I'm sure. His face—the hollows, the lines—were always (and remain) so infinitely moving. I can't help feeling sad.

I had almost finished *The Shackle,* a love story that happened to be set in the Riviera, when we left Provence. "To speak of love is to speak of the future," the heroine says before she gets caught. The French moralists were filled with aphorisms on this subject, but they usually weren't uttered by a woman. Unfortunately, my life wasn't a novel—by Colette or anyone else. And I couldn't stay in a story without a future.

I dreaded seeing Jim, but we had to deal with the car. The Austin had given us problems from the beginning, even on the honeymoon. Neither of us wanted it anymore. The car's breakdowns had come to represent the failure of the marriage. The symbolism was too obvious for either of us to miss.

We met at the café downstairs from the apartment. It felt a little like returning to the scene of the crime, but then all of Paris was heavy with memory, including the car that had marked our arrival as a couple on the rise. Jim was waiting for me at his usual table in the back. Seeing him at a distance, I remembered meeting him for my second interview at Ruc, when he had hired me to work for him four years earlier. He hadn't changed very much, I thought, physically at least, and yet everything else had. We couldn't figure out how to greet each other, and settled on the *bise,* feigning French civility, kissing the air.

"What do you want to do with the car?"

"I'll take it to the Austin dealer, let them fix it and then sell it for whatever they can get."

"What about your business trips?"

"I'll go back to renting." Jim looked weary. "I still have the scooter for Paris."

The Austin dealer was located outside Paris in a suburb reached through the *boulevards périphériques,* the heavily traveled roads that encircle the city. Jim would rent a car from an agency near the apartment. I would follow in the Austin. Once we had left our ailing car in the garage, he would drive me back to Paris in the rental.

We met in front of the café the following day.

It was tricky enough getting out of the city, but once we entered the fast-paced circuit of the outer boulevards I started to panic. I gripped the steering wheel and stared straight ahead as I tried to follow Jim's lead. I was afraid of losing him as he changed lanes, weaving in and out of the speeding traffic. A car passed me on my right and honked insistently. Then something happening on my left caught my attention and I turned my head slightly. A Peugeot moving in the opposite direction had jumped the dividing line and was heading rapidly, unswervingly, toward the little green car my parents had bought us. It just kept coming, like an action shot in a B-movie chase. I closed my eyes, braced my arms against the steering wheel, and pushed the brake to the floor. At that moment, in the fraction of the second it took the thought to form, the words of the cliché appeared like a balloon over the head of a cartoon character: "My life is over!" Calm spread through my body like the rush of a Valium drip. Then the crash shocked me back into ordinary consciousness. I opened my eyes, looked at the cars around me, and saw myself planted in the center of a five-car pileup. The front end of the Austin was completely smashed in, the fenders crumpled like used Kleenex. I saw myself sitting there, wedged neatly between the seat and the dashboard, intact. I had smashed my forehead against the steering wheel, but I was able to move.

How could it have happened? The story started to emerge from different witnesses, all gesticulating and shouting. The Peugeot's steering wheel had locked as the driver was trying to pass the vehicle in front of him. The car became a ballistic missile aimed involuntarily at a vulnerable target. A traffic cop threaded his way through the wreckage and carefully reached in to extract me from the front seat of the Austin, where I was still sitting, stunned. I looked down and noticed that the dress I was wearing rode up my thighs as I climbed out of the totaled car. I was wearing a spring dress for my dinner that evening with Dominique, a short, straight, wool shift in an orange-and-white houndstooth pattern I had chosen to show off my tan. It seemed frivolous to care, but I couldn't help noticing. I knew Dominique would appreciate the detail when I told her about the accident.

As the policeman led me over to the ambulance, my mood swung from dazed to giddy. When I looked back at the pileup, I could not believe I had survived. On the way to the hospital for X-rays, I mentally scanned my underwear. The doctors in the crowded emergency room were briefly interested in the egg-like lump that had popped out in the center of my forehead. A radiologist read the results and told me that I was very lucky. I should see my doctor for a follow-up when I got to Paris. Jim turned up at the hospital as I was being released and drove me back to my hotel. The insurance papers for the car were at the apartment, he said. He would be in touch. The loving persona of his letters to me while I was away in the south of France was gone. Now that I was present and real, I knew he was determined to punish me however he could, and I felt unable to blame him.

LATER THAT NIGHT I VISITED Dominique in her apartment near the Luxembourg Gardens. Dominique had always seemed to me the epitome of Parisian stylishness. She didn't look like a professor—she made a point of never dressing like one, she had told me one day, a rule I've tried to follow. A beaky nose kept her face from being perfect, but her tall, slender body exuded sexiness. She wore Guerlain's "L'heure bleue," a musky, powdery perfume that permeated her clothes, clung to her scarves, and made me dizzy. You could almost taste the scent in the air. I asked to try some. Dominique, who was in her early forties, said I was much too young for "L'heure bleue." We sat cross-legged on the floor of her apartment on the rue Racine and drank shots of Johnny Walker Black Label. We almost finished the bottle as I told her about the accident. She laughed about the dress and said I should wear slacks more often.

"You were right about Mark. He told me he preferred the company of women but was attracted to men. He said it was his neurosis. What does that mean?"

"It means you shouldn't have slept with him."

"He accused me of self-deception, of not knowing my feelings. He had analyzed our time together in his mind, and the only thing he could think of that he had done wrong was to let himself get into a position where I could hurt him!"

"Did you really think he was going to be honest with you?"

We finished the bottle. I could feel that I didn't want to leave and that Dominique didn't want me to either.

"You look adorable sitting there. You tempt me, but you've been through too much today. Another time."

We kissed goodnight. I walked back to my hotel room, past the closed iron gates of the Luxembourg Gardens, past the deserted square in front of the Pantheon, wishing I had stayed to be comforted, and taking in—maybe not quite—what Dominique had just revealed to me. Adorable. Another time?

Staying would have been a turning point, but I had missed the turn.

The next day I made grim faces in a Photomaton in case we needed proof of injury for the car insurance. I drew a self-portrait with colored pens to show my parents what my eyes looked like: violet lids with yellowing circles under them. I couldn't figure out how to show the lump. Later in the week, I met Jim at the Coupole to discuss the car insurance. The driver was claiming it was my fault.

"My fault!" I put my head in my hands. Maybe it was.

The Minotaur

FROM THE LITTLE HOUSE HE had rented on the Turkish coast, Mark dithered endlessly about meeting me in Greece. I could tell from his letters how much he enjoyed keeping me dangling. I finally booked my flight without knowing. Once I got to Athens, I was relieved to learn he wouldn't join me, after all. Except for the permanent shadow operations of the young Greek men, who were relentless in their pursuit of foreign women on their own, I was happy to be without a companion.

At Knossos, the guide explained the legend of King Minos and the Minotaur at the heart of the labyrinth. While he was asking us to imagine the vanished civilization from the arrangements of the fragments that remained, my mind drifted back to the apartment Jim and I had bought with so much hope for our future. Could history be reconstructed from the floor plans he had sketched? I was beginning to think that my first mistake was a literary one. Lennie and George never get the ranch. That was the whole point. Jim and I both knew how the story turned out in the novel. The ranch should have remained a metaphor; we had been much too literal. Whatever else, ancient ruins put the present mess into perspective, which didn't make it any easier to bear. I seemed to have moved inward in ever tighter circles, instead of out into a discernible line that I could follow on the horizon.

What eluded me was a pattern in the carpet, except the one proposed by Dr. Mendelsohn. Here in the land of Oedipus I couldn't help thinking about our sessions. I was tired of talking about my parents and me. It was enough that I had to deal with them in the present by letter. I didn't see why everything should be explained by some archaic, universal family psychodrama—about a son, no less. True, my life thus far had been a series of miserable failures; was the only way out to dig deeper into that dark material?

Back at Hotel Iraklion after the tour, I lay on my bed and went through the mail. Like the chorus in a Greek play announcing future woes and lamenting errors past, each letter that I opened brought me fresh expressions of disapproval, except from Jonathan, who had plans to reappear in Paris and take me out to dinner. He wanted to see my suntan. I wrote back to warn him he was going to be disappointed; I had already started to peel. Getting tan, I explained, figuring he'd like the analogy, was just the objective correlative of my self-defeating efforts at self-transformation. Trying to be someone else, someone, precisely, who tanned and didn't just get burned. The traces of the accident were taking longer to disappear than the doctor had predicted, and I still had very dark circles under my eyes.

My father was enjoying his role as paterfamilias. The name of the monster in the labyrinth was obvious. He followed the money, and the money provided the thread out of the maze. Jim not only had failed to make good on the business and to provide for me as husbands are meant to do, but he had presented himself to my father as someone he wasn't. My father had reluctantly accepted the fact of his daughter marrying a non-Jew. His generosity of spirit should have been rewarded, not betrayed. Fueling his anger about the loss of the money—the money he had loaned us for the apartment, the money he thought Jim owed me—was something deeper, if unacknowledged, including to Jim, the man who had conned Mr. Just-Give-Me-The-Facts. The best my father could hope for now was to keep others from knowing what he knew: "Don't sound off unnecessarily to anyone. After all, it's no one's business but our own." I translated his anxiety back into the Yiddish word I heard in everything he said, even if he couldn't bring himself to give voice to the shame—the *shonda* that Jewish families dread having exposed to the world at large.

Shame. First my sister had shamed the family by living with a Negro. Andrea said he was Puerto Rican. A Puerto Rican Negro might even be worse. Now I was getting divorced. Where would it end? What would people say? This time the word my father wanted was not in Yiddish, but German: schadenfreude, joy in the suffering of others. People would enjoy pitying my parents. I felt bad about the money—and guilty. I doubted Jim would ever pay my father back. It would be years before I could do so (not that they wanted the money from me, mad and disappointed as they were). But I hated the immigrant subtext of keeping it all in the family. Don't tell; don't tell anyone. It made me want to shout it from the rooftops, like Jane Eyre, declaring her right to exist. "Anybody may blame me who likes."

For once, my mother, who usually led the charge in the assaults on my character, stayed out of the fray, letting my father treat me as an incipient legal case. I could see my name on one of his long manila folders, maybe even one of those brick-colored accordion containers that were the repository for the mysteries of his practice that had haunted my childhood. "I'm reserving my annoyance for when I see you" was point number three out of eleven in a two-page letter telling me how to conduct the rest of my life: "It's a tolerable world if one takes Polonius's advice. Just memorize that philosophy." I did not want to hear from Polonius, whom my father never saw as the pompous character he was. I was angry at my father for not guessing how hard it all was.

"You must remember that I live daily, hourly, constantly with guilt and worries about the future. It's not easy to be me right now," I replied. "The accident was the finishing touch. Knowing how fragile my mental health is, how can you seriously *plan* to take a critical position?" Why couldn't my father try to see the situation from my point of view, I wondered, instead of spouting clichés from Shakespeare, probably culled from *Bartlett's Familiar Quotations,* which was where he found most of his maxims? His favorite line from Polonius's recommendations for getting along in what he always called the real world, "To thine own self be true," was taken up by Mark in a fancier, Sartrean gear: "You cheat yourself of the truth the better to cheat others." I made another note in my diary for Dr. Mendelsohn, whom I had reluctantly decided to see when I returned to New York. He said it was important to put labels on things. I filed this under Superior Man Syndrome.

The truth was, I didn't know what the truth was. And the legends didn't help. Unlike my father, I couldn't so easily identify the monster at the heart of the labyrinth. I couldn't slay the monster like Theseus, no more than I could offer a thread to a rescuer like Ariadne. The monster, I often felt, was me.

Sitting alone at café tables in the sun, I obsessively rehearsed the collapse of the marriage in my diary: "Would things have been all right between us if I still had been working or was it H.? He seemed so necessary, but in other circumstances . . ." I trailed off, desperate for answers, looking as always to the heroines of my favorite novels. Would Emma Bovary have had the disastrous affairs that led her to suicide if she had held down a full-time job? Anna Karenina? No, married women had affairs and tried to kill themselves, if I was any example, because they didn't have enough to do. And, my mother would have added had we debated the matter, because they didn't get enough exercise. A couple of tough sets of singles would have absorbed the energy that was looking for trouble. The flaw in the analysis was that tennis (if I played, which naturally I didn't) left my constant companions dread and its twin demon, longing, in place. Besides, I wasn't looking for trouble, as my mother liked to say. I found trouble in place of what I was looking for. I had answered an ad for teachers of English and found a husband. I had hired a carpenter to convert our apartment into my husband's school and succumbed to a literary cliché.

Now that I was almost sans husband, past the threshold of repair, my father was determined to get everything straightened out. This tactic didn't work with Jim, who thought in wavy lines and who refused in twisty prose to respond to my father's direct questions. Learning how to manipulate French bureaucracy had made Jim an expert at evading the law. He had once boasted to Alain about having talked a tax collector into taking English lessons in exchange for an extension on his payment schedule. Far from feeling guilty or remiss, Jim expected sympathy from my father and complained to him that I was the one creating impediments to resolving our affairs.

My father could not fathom why I wasn't helping in the campaign for a financial settlement. In his view, I was entitled to a substantial financial settlement, if not alimony. But I felt like Anna Karenina: I expected punishment, not economic reward.

> *Jim has his faults and his quirks BUT don't forget— I broke up the marriage, I left, and until I did there was nothing objectionable (on any official scale) in his behavior. That we were short of money is not a crime. No law says he had to support me in high style. Things are finished between us, all right. I'll do something legal about it when the time comes. But you know, from the European point of view, I was wrong. I left and created the state of tension that was responsible for subsequent unpleasantness. Which is to say: don't be hard on him. Above all, wait—I'm a long, long way from needing my freedom on those terms.*

I wasn't trying to absolve Jim of responsibility: he owed my father the money because they had made a business deal and I thought Jim should pay him back. I was trying to get my father off the case because I couldn't explain why I felt guilty. As far as my father was concerned, in choosing Jim I had made an error of judgment, thus confirming his original view of the man. Fortunately, I had come to my senses. To explain how my unexpected discovery of sexual passion—my second error of judgment—had torpedoed the scheme he had bankrolled was not part of the analysis.

Despite the acrimony that had started permeating their correspondence, Jim and my father continued to write to each other. My father had never confronted Jim with the lies he had uncovered at Easter time about the unfinished BA. I persuaded my father that it would only enrage Jim, increase his paranoia, to bring up the subject. Instead, they discussed the situation in the Middle East, man-to-man, in the aftermath of the Six-Day War. Jim announced that as a Jew by marriage, he needed to make clear, in case my father was wondering, that he was profoundly anti-Zionist. "I am *not*, repeat, *not* a Zionist," my father echoed, as if bonding with his son-in-law. Jim devised a few suggestions for Israel's future that included the merging of Israel and Jordan with King Hussein as president of the Republic. My father did not reply to Jim's ideas about how to solve the crisis in the Middle East, though, infuriated by de Gaulle's declared neutrality about the war, in the summer of 1967 he saved his shekels, as he put it, and, in a grand but useless gesture, boycotted France.

"Qu'est-ce que c'est, dégueulasse?"

A MESSAGE FROM NATHALIE, MY friend from the lycée days, was waiting for me at the hotel when I returned to Paris: "Jim has had a very serious scooter accident. Call me." While I was in the south of France, Nathalie and Jim had started seeing each other. It was my idea, in fact, the last gasp of my eighteenth-century fantasies about manipulating other people into stories of my making. When I moved out of the apartment at the end of May, I took Nathalie to dinner and told her I thought she and Jim might do well together. He had that huge apartment. He always wanted a child. She had a child without a father.

"I find him really intimidating; he seems to know everything."

"It's mainly bluff. He makes it up as he goes along. Anyway, the only thing he really cares about is food."

"That's part of what worries me."

I proposed that the three of us go out to dinner together when I returned to Paris, but in the meantime, to follow two basic rules and she'd be fine: always order a vegetable as an appetizer, and never skip the cheese course.

After I said good-bye to Nathalie, I was overcome by sadness. I was leaving. She was going to live at the ranch.

I told Mark about my dinner with Nathalie. He said it was a cruel thing to do to a friend. People weren't literary characters for me to move around. Why was I pushing someone I cared for into a relationship with someone with whom I had almost lost my life, or wanted to, at least? Why did I think she would be happy with Jim when I had been so miserable?

"She's tougher than I am. She's a mother. Maybe she'll figure out how to make it work."

By leaving Jim the apartment, by putting Nathalie in my place, I was giving him the chance to have the ranch without me. He could still make the school happen if he wanted to, I said. The last few months didn't have to be fatal to his dream.

I didn't have to feel guilty about falling out of love and wanting what I couldn't have with him.

NATHALIE AND I MET AT a Vietnamese restaurant near my hotel.

"What happened?"

"He doesn't remember anything. He has a fractured skull and broken ribs. He has to lie completely still for ten days. Then there will be three days of observation."

"I'd like to see him."

"He doesn't want you to come to the hospital."

"Why? He's been writing me endless letters."

"You know how he is."

I wasn't sure how far to go in telling Nathalie what I had learned about Jim. "You know how he is" meant she already understood the bargain she had struck.

"So you stay with Jim," I said finally over jasmine tea, "and have another child." Nathalie smiled but looked sad. I knew she was wondering whether I had regrets about not having had a child with Jim, and about the life in Paris I was giving up.

"Do you think you'll like the teaching job in New York?" she asked, almost politely.

"No, I'm sure I'll hate it, but at least I'll be busy."

"Busy is better than Valium." Nathalie smiled again. It was one of her best lines.

JIM LOOKED FRAGILE UNDER THE white bandage that swathed his square head.

"I told Nathalie I didn't want to see you," he said angrily. Nathalie and I exchanged glances. You know how he is.

"There isn't any money, you know. I owe everybody."

Jim closed his eyes. I thought he might have gone to sleep.

"I brought you a book," I said, finally.

"What?" he asked, his voice flat.

"*A Spaniard in the Works.* John Lennon's second book. I saw it in the window of Shakespeare and Company. I don't think you have it."

"Nathalie doesn't know anything about books," Jim said.

"She'll learn," I said, holding on to the last shreds of conjugal complicity between us.

Jim had closed his eyes again. Nathalie pulled the curtains around his bed. I felt grateful to her for being there, in the place I had vacated, without ever fully knowing why.

She walked me slowly to the door of the hospital room and we kissed good-bye for the last time as friends.

I left Paris for New York the next day.

AT THE END OF *BREATHLESS,* when Jean-Paul Belmondo lies dying on his back in the street, he looks up at Jean Seberg, who has betrayed him. "Dégueulasse," he says as life drains out of him.

"Dégueulasse," she queries the policeman watching the scene,

"Qu'est-ce que c'est, dégueulasse?" The policeman says the word means she is "disgusting."

When I first saw the film with David in New York, I was proud of having a better vocabulary in French than Jean Seberg. I knew what Belmondo meant without the subtitles.

When I walked away from Jim in the hospital, I couldn't help feeling that the word now described me.

Paris in New York

I WAS BACK IN NEW York for good, sharing an apartment on the Upper East Side with a stranger—Karina Heath, a girl my age who needed a roommate—and teaching French at a high school in an expensive part of Westchester. Karina resembled the neighborhood women in style, if not income: blue blazer and Gucci loafers (also blue), Black Watch plaid, pleated skirt. She deftly tied an Hermès scarf over her straight, streaky blonde hair every morning on her way to work in a large mid-town travel agency, buoyed by that inimitable air of WASP sublime that only her bad English boyfriend could dent. Kevin had commitment issues. He also smoked in the shower.

The rent-controlled apartment at 4 East 74th Street had been home to a succession of young hopefuls who had come to Manhattan to find work, while also dreaming, like the career girls in Rona Jaffe's *The Best of Everything*, of finding love. The layout of the miniature two-bedroom apartment on the top floor was perfect for sharing. You entered directly

into a long hallway. The kitchen, barely the size of a closet (which it originally was), was off to the right, followed by the bathroom, and then, an
unexpected European touch, a separate toilet. At the end of the hallway
was the living room (which was also the dining room), and through it,
Karina's bedroom. Just opposite the kitchen was my minuscule bedroom.
Its windows were covered with iron gates and heavy drapes because they
faced onto the narrow terrace of a duplex apartment occupied by an heir
(tall, WASP, and blond like Karina) to a family fortune (the grandparents had created a famous brand of mattress) comparable to that of the
Stetsons, for whom the limestone townhouse had been designed at the
turn of the century. At 3 AM, his guests smoked and laughed on the terrace outside my window.

I lived in my sunless room like a solitary cave dweller.

When I returned to America in the fall of 1967, I resembled a work
in progress, I thought on my better days, trying to emphasize the forward
motion. But I had spent more of my so-called adult life in Paris than in
New York and I was still attached to Paris by loose ends that I could
neither tie up nor sever. I might have changed continents, but Paris kept
arriving by mail.

In late September, I received a letter from Dr. Hirsch, my gynecologist. When I said good-bye to him in Paris, he told me that he might
be spending a few days in New York for a medical convention. "It would
give me pleasure (if it is shared)," he wrote in the elegant handwriting I
recognized from my prescriptions, "in having dinner with you, or at least
to meet, if you are free." The caveat of reciprocity embedded in the paren-
theses was endearingly humble, considering the fact that the man was a
doctor and French. I appreciated the courtesy, even though I assumed
that once I said yes to dinner, he would expect me to go to his room
afterward and share that pleasure too.

I dialed the Americana Hotel and left a message with the operator
saying I would meet Dr. Hirsch at the restaurant in the hotel lobby
the following evening. I could hear the nervousness in my voice. I was
relieved to have missed him. As soon as I put the receiver down, I
wanted to pick it up again to cancel. I was flattered by the invitation
and curious about the man who was, after all, a pioneer in the medical

world, but what, really, was I going to find out? How many more experiments did I need to convince myself that I was—what was I? Attractive? Or was I just available? There was still time to take it back. There
was always coffee.

That June in Provence I read an Aldous Huxley novel Jim had sent
me from Paris. I wasn't sure why—he always had a didactic reason for his
literary recommendations—but I had noted down a quotation from the
main character's diary in my own. "Like all other human beings, I know
what I ought to do, but continue to do what I know I oughtn't to do." I
had trouble not doing what I knew I shouldn't do. But how could I be
sure I didn't want to without trying? That reasoning wouldn't wash with
Dr. Mendelsohn, but for the time being, I was still gathering experience
to submit for inspection.

I hadn't committed to change, only to thinking about what should
change.

At dinner, the conversation languished between courses. The doctor
had seemed more alluring when we tried to talk past the awkwardness
imposed by the probe of the latex-gloved hand. An office visit, unlike
dinner, was a matter of carefully calculated minutes of attention. Maybe
you couldn't eliminate the stirrups and the speculum at the heart of the
relationship. By the time the waiter arrived with the check, we were eating in silence. The doctor cleared his throat and pushed his half-eaten
dessert to the side. I lit a cigarette and waited warily, wondering how
he'd make his next move. He picked up the check as well as my hand
across the table.

"Chère amie," he finally said, gazing into my eyes, "I have a wonderful view of the city from my room." It wasn't as if I imagined Dr. Hirsch
(as I continued to think of him, even though he had asked me to call him
Pierre) wanted to discuss the results of my fertility tests in depth.

"You know it's late." Why couldn't I have left his letter unanswered?
"I leave for work very early in the morning." Dr. Hirsch frowned the way
he did in the office when he palpated something unexpected with his
long fingers.

"I suppose I could come up just for a minute," I said, resigned to the
evening's inevitable denouement, which would also entail admitting that

I seemed to have developed an infection over the summer. I knew the appropriate vocabulary, but when I imagined the balloon dialogue over my head, those words did not fit the space. I let the doctor usher me into the elevator.

The view of Manhattan skyscrapers at night from the thirty-second floor of the Americana Hotel resembled the romantic skyline of movie trailers. After contemplating the spectacle of the bright city lights from the window for a while, honoring the fiction of the view, we sat down on the bed. Without speaking, the doctor pushed me gently back on the bedspread and moved to kiss me. I loosened his tie and opened his shirt at the collar. His chest was surprisingly smooth. All his hair seemed concentrated in his very thick mustache. As Dr. Hirsch stretched out next to me, his long legs dangling over the edge of the mattress, I speculated about how old he was, what he liked to do, but most of all, when, despite the familiar throb of curiosity our proximity had produced, I was going to come clean.

He laughed when I told him, though I could hear a slight choke of irritation in his voice. "That happens a lot with women on the pill," he said in doctor mode, "especially in hot weather." Even so, he gallantly slipped his hand under my skirt and caressed me expertly, professionally, I thought later, worthy of a gynecologist. I gestured toward returning the favor, remembering what he had said about shared pleasure. "Another time," he said gently, both of us knowing the moment had passed, and put the cab fare in my hand. I forgot to ask him about my test results.

Dr. Hirsch was the first man I had been to bed with since the fiasco with Mark. This was a fiasco in its own right, of course, and "bed" a figure of speech, but I was relieved that I could still *plaire*—that irregular verb whose meaning I had finally understood: the turn-on minus love, and sometimes even affection. I had also begun to understand that *plaire* would take me only so far on the map of tenderness, certainly not to a place of happiness.

1968

In February, right before my birthday, I applied to graduate school at Columbia, in part because more school was always my remedy for despair, and in part because Dominique, sending New Year's wishes from Paris and bored with my installments of epistolary misery, had challenged me: Why Mark (who had entered a PhD program already) and not you? she wanted to know. I had always thought the PhD was a boyfriend affair: David would get a doctorate. I could marry one. Why not be like Dominique instead, free and independent, with an apartment of my own? Dominique didn't offer herself as a model, of course, but the example of her career helped me see past the door I had closed out of fear. True, most of the professors at the university were men, but not all. She taught American literature at the university in France. I could live Dominique's life in reverse.

I was already enamored of her perfume and her perfectly tied scarves.

As I fanned out the documents on the bed, I felt crushed by the disparity between the girl on paper and the other me gathering evidence. Viewed through the categories of a curriculum vitae, the last six years looked like an almost uninterrupted stream of academic accomplishment. I had gathered the names of well-known professors willing to write enthusiastic letters of recommendation from France. I could even list the book with Couderc as a future publication (no one needed to know how unlikely that actually was). But if she was something (serial degrees), I was nothing (serial men).

I was an ex-heroine with an ex-husband, a girl without a plot. My list of boyfriends, lovers, and even husband was the narrative of my sentimental education in France, abruptly brought to an unhappy ending.

On the last Sunday in March, I was sitting on the floor of my room polishing my shoes for school, watching television and drinking vodka. Sunday nights were always the hardest, even with the vodka-Valium cocktail I had perfected, a numbing balanced out by the jolt of Ritalin in the morning. I loved my little nine-inch black-and-white Zenith, the first television set I had ever owned. Television, I quickly discovered, was the perfect partner, the ideal companion for the weekend nights alone, when my roommate Karina went to Vermont with her boyfriend, and the apartment filled with her absence. Suddenly, Lyndon Johnson appeared on the small screen. In his address to the nation, Johnson sorrowfully declared that he would not be the Democratic Party candidate for president in the fall elections. He announced a pause in the American bombing of Vietnam. Johnson's sense of personal failure looked like a turning point in the story of the war that until now the administration had presented as almost won. I imagined the crowing of French intellectuals, the headlines in *Le Monde,* as if the casualties of the American quagmire erased the memory of France's own bloody battles in Indochina.

The president's address caused a momentary ripple of political optimism about ending the war. Even I felt a brief lift of hopefulness through the fog of my own despair. I drained my glass of vodka-on-the-rocks in the darkened room.

Later that week, in early April, Martin Luther King, Jr., was assassinated.

I taught my classes in intermediate French as if nothing had happened. The required textbook featured dialogues between "Jean" and his younger sister "Marie." They lived on a farm in Normandy. Except for the parents of "Jean" and "Marie," the other characters were mainly cows and the occasional Camembert. The students had no vocabulary for death or race—we were living in Normandy, after all, where everything ran as smoothly as ripe cheese—and politics, the principal had already explained to me during my interview, did not belong in the classroom.

The demands of teaching French at a fancy public high school in Westchester proved to be almost exactly what I had imagined, dreaded, and, in a way, needed. The vocation of high school teacher was precisely the nice-Jewish-girl fate I'd hoped to escape by moving to France, but I was forced to recognize that the daily preparation for the long hours of high school teaching, compounded by the extra time the commute to the suburbs entailed, absorbed some of the spreading panic the breakup with Jim had set free. An existence with no time for feeling was what I wanted. "I must stay busy," I underlined in my diary, "or havoc sets in." I had signed the contract in the countryside of Provence as I listened to the cry of the cicadas. There, I was afraid not to. The position at Chappaqua was also the only one I had found open in my frantic visit to New York the previous Easter.

I was teaching, it often seemed, the grammar of something I had lived when I was someone else—when I believed in the ranch. In part, my confusion was a matter of tenses. The *passé simple*, the definite, literary past of completion and fiction, the simple past in which the narrative of my French life was over, was now the *passé composé*, the indefinite past tense of ordinary human activity, where beginnings and endings sometimes shade into each other. Despite the drama of the overdose, my life had not ended in the little back room of the unfinished apartment. Still, I couldn't see even the outline of a new story. I felt like the reduction of a former self I no longer recognized, but not like the reduction of a French sauce that by dint of cooking becomes more intense. No, I was diluted—or maybe just stretched too thin, attenuated by the teaching and the drugs.

My favorite student in the Intermediate French class wrote me a letter about what the death of Martin Luther King, Jr. had meant to her. The woman she thought of as her mother, the woman who had taken care of her when her own mother died, was black. Sarah described this woman as a figure of love. She mourned the lost dream of racial harmony. She said she could tell, even though we hadn't discussed it in class, that King's murder had upset me, too.

Soon after, in the early days of June, Bobby Kennedy was shot and killed.

During final exams, Sarah wrote again, this time to say good-bye— she was moving to Los Angeles because of her father's career in television; she hoped things would go better for me. I was doing the right thing in leaving the high school, she said. She knew I wanted something else.

By the time I returned to France in August and collected my belongings from the apartment Jim had kept, the events of May 1968 in Paris had become part of France's revolutionary mythology. Traces of the upheaval still could be read on the city's walls. "The more I make revolution, the more I make love." The scrawled yearnings of youthful desire, sometimes witty, sometimes obscure, kept the memory of hopefulness alive. I prowled the bookstores in the Latin Quarter where the students had rioted when the police invaded the territory of the Sorbonne. Books about the events of May and souvenirs were proliferating, already objects of kitsch, like little Eiffel Towers, as though what had happened only months before was already history. The Sorbonne, where I had spent many hours taking notes during lectures, had become a symbol of political dissent—the courtyard a battleground of warring forces. It was obvious from the books alone that the effects of the student rebellion would last beyond the actual violence. So would the memory of the burned-out Citroëns whose battered carcasses had dotted the devastated neighborhood landscape, images captured in the black-and-white photographs that were also for sale. I bought posters recycling the graffiti of revolution: TAKE PLEASURE WITHOUT LIMITS. FORBIDDEN TO FORBID.

I planned to tack the posters on the walls of my bedroom in New York.

Mai soixante-huit. May 1968. A date almost instantly, internationally magical made the idea of my going to graduate school at Columbia, where I had been accepted into the French department, seem sexy. The student occupation of administration buildings at Columbia that spring had taken place almost simultaneously with the events in Paris. On television, from my room, I had watched, lying in bed, anesthetized but fascinated, the police invade the campus I had crossed many times, always feeling intimidated, as though as a Barnard girl I didn't quite belong on that side of the street. I wished I had been there, emblazoned with a black armband, standing on the steps of Low Library in solidarity with my fellow students, and dreamed of dressing like a revolutionary.

Before I left Paris, I bought a pair of jeans with an inset of soft black suede that ran down the front of the legs and up into the crotch: a French interpretation of American blue jeans. The pants were already broken in and looked as though their owner had spent time on a ranch. Urban cowgirl after the reign of LBJ. Perfect for classes in the fall.

I hadn't surrendered the keys to the apartment when I moved out, but I was sure that Jim had changed the locks. I waited on the landing for Nathalie to let me in. I had become a guest in my own home. Jim would not speak to me, and Nathalie had arranged for me to come to the apartment one afternoon while he was teaching. I noticed her paella pan on the stove. I didn't resent her presence exactly. After all, I had chosen to leave and chosen her, as I liked to tell people, as my replacement. She was my hedge against total guilt. At the same time, there was something just a little too easy about this calculus according to which Nathalie acquired a father for her daughter, Jim found a new wife, and the happy family got to live in the two hundred square meters my parents had leased for Jim's fantasy language school. My father had subsidized the disaster in dollars, as he never failed to mention whenever the subject of the marriage came up. The cost to me was less easy to assess because I was still struggling with the turn everything had taken. In the beginning, when he thought the marriage still had a chance of survival, Jim had assumed some of the blame. Gradually I became solely responsible. My leaving eclipsed all faults of his, from lies to drinking to the financial ruin of the company.

As I wandered through the apartment, packing the stone menorah made in Israel and the antique candle snuffer from my cousins into an empty suitcase, I could no longer remember why I had been so determined to retrieve the wedding presents from a marriage beyond saving. All spring, Jim and I had argued by mail about what was mine and what was his. (Wedding gifts from my family were a priori mine: including my copy of *The Joy of Cooking* and a complete set, not that a set was ever complete, of blue-and-white Corning Ware casserole dishes.) Jim would keep the floor-to-ceiling cherry bookshelves; in exchange he would let me take the Spanish dining room table.

Nathalie told me that H., whose name had become a precious initial in my private shorthand, was still in town. I had no wish to see him again. I had always known he was the accident in my path, not the path. But his presence was palpable throughout the winding labyrinth of rooms, especially in the back of the apartment, when I was his "little fish." I could see where he had repaired the floorboards that Jim had ripped out in rage. I admired the new kitchen counter he had built. I said good-bye again to Nathalie at the threshold of the apartment. We kissed each other on the cheeks, as sadly as lovers who meet after the end of an affair only to part again.

I loved Paris, even in August, when real Parisians had left town. Cabs cruised everywhere and you could have a chair in the sun at the Deux Magots, if you didn't mind sitting next to camera-toting Americans. I had already become a tourist.

Crossing Broadway

WHEN I FIRST WENT TO Paris, I was younger than everyone I knew. By the time I entered graduate school, the six years of my twenties that I had spent in Paris suddenly became a gap, a blank in American chronology that I never filled in without alluding darkly to my European past. I had forfeited my role as ingénue. Compared to some of the students who had just graduated from college, I could easily pass for a woman of the world, the fantasy identity that had eluded me in Paris. I didn't like feeling old, and yet I couldn't completely regret the journey. I had proved to myself that I could get married—as important as losing one's virginity at an earlier stage. I could count the number of my lovers on my fingers. I knew how to say, not to mention do, things in French that young women my age were not supposed to have in their repertoire. (That made me alternately proud and embarrassed.) I was a minor expert in French cheese and wine.

There was more, I thought, looking back. Despite the epistolary chains, I had lived far from home on Riverside Drive. At times I might have seemed to resemble Penelope, waiting for my wandering hero to return, but I too had had my odyssey, heard the songs of the sirens, dallied with Circe, if these things were reversible. But maybe the *Odyssey* was not the right literary model, no more than *Les Liaisons Dangereuses*, for what I was trying to do. I still didn't know what was.

From my years on the Barnard side, Columbia seemed contained and bounded on the east side of Broadway, its entrance marked by wrought-iron gates, as, of course, was Barnard's. I had crossed Broadway at 116th Street many times when I was an undergraduate, but Broadway then was so much more than a New York street to cross. The Columbia side of the street was David's way, not mine. In 1968 the distance between Barnard and Columbia that once had seemed immense shrank to the size of the mere urban avenue that separated the two schools. You still had to watch out for the traffic, but the distance lacked symbolic dimensions.

When I strolled into my first graduate seminar dressed in my tight Parisian jeans, I wondered why it had taken me so long to get there. All I needed to do was cross the street.

In my application to graduate school I said I wanted to concentrate on eighteenth-century literature. I chose that period because it had so much to teach us, I explained, about the desire for individual freedom. I wanted, though I didn't say it because I couldn't have said it then, to stop trying to live in books and to write about them instead. Ultimately, I completed a very long dissertation about eighteenth-century novels of seduction and betrayal and coldly analyzed the destiny of the unhappy heroines who had held me in thrall during my Parisian interlude. After a while, my life in fiction became an object of study, as I became a professor of French literature.

"After a while" sounds a bit too much like a fairy tale to account for the academic rites of passage, as well as the struggle to believe that there was someone or something to become, and not just a blind hope for yet another romance (not that I had given up on romance) or marriage. As the 1960s morphed into the 1970s, I finally started to figure out that it was time for something new. But it required a leap of faith, and the invention of feminism, for a girl who had grown up in the 1950s to imagine herself as a professor, as a person having a profession. What seems harder to believe now is that I had lived so many years without realizing that if I was ever going to be happy (or at least not desperately miserable), I needed to do something, not just be someone—least of all, someone's wife (not that I had given up on that, either).

Epilogue: Out of Breath

PARIS IN THE 1960s WAS full of Americans suffering from the disease of imitation. Jim, who couldn't write, took himself for James Joyce in exile from a country that his parents had already left. Jim thought marrying a Jew would save him from the priests. I thought marrying him would save me from the rabbis. In some ways, Dr. Mendelsohn was right: Jim was not the worst choice I could have made. But we were so busy using each other in order to avoid our fates that we missed recognizing who *else* we were—what we wanted from the world when we weren't reading books, or eating. I couldn't stay married to someone who was making up everything all the time, including me.

My copycat adventures had always been doomed to failure because that was precisely what had to happen for me to grow up. The point I kept missing—and that got me in trouble—was that whatever I was going to become, or however I was going to become someone, required my not imitating someone else. Wasn't that really the lesson of *Breathless*? It's not for nothing that the movie begins with Belmondo copying Bogart's trademark gesture of passing his thumb over his lips. Belmondo's character Michel can't even make it as a successful hood, as my father would have said then. I might have followed Jean Seberg as Patricia to France, the way other, more literary (and nicer) girls followed Henry James's Isabel Archer to England, but after that start, I was on my own for the rest of the plot.

At the end of *Breathless*, Seberg walks away from the scene of the crime. The movie doesn't let us know whether her character will ever write her novel, whether she'll go home again after she finishes school at the Sorbonne to please her parents, who are paying for it, or just keep selling the *New York Herald Tribune* until the next man comes along—we already know she won't have to wait long. We don't find out whether she's really pregnant or what she'll do about it. But we figure she'll make out. That's one of the things about this American girl and why I liked her so much: she thrives on experience, no matter how devastating.

À bout de souffle, the expression in the French title of the movie that had set me gasping after experience, means two things: breathless with anticipation and out of breath. Between the time I saw the movie in New York and the time I returned from Paris, I had exhausted the dictionary definition. In Europe I thought I would rid myself of the American girl rooted in me and be free. I didn't turn into the person other than myself I thought I wanted to become. I wasn't sure how to grow out of what had failed to happen. As in the dream where you keep panting as you try to move forward but find yourself running in place, in the end I ran out of breath.

HANS DIED OF A STROKE that probably was due to a heroin overdose—Leo wasn't sure. At sixty-five, cool as ever, Leo opened a jazz bar in Montparnasse, fulfilling the ultimate hip expatriate dream. Jonathan remarried and died of a heart attack a few years ago. Sarah opened a school for martial arts in Chicago.

Around the time that Hans died, Jean Seberg was found dead in the backseat of her car in Paris. The police reported a large dose of barbiturates in her system. Some say the FBI hounded her to death. She is buried in the cemetery at Montparnasse, near Leo's bar, near where I first lived with Jim; Beauvoir and Sartre are buried there, too. The American girl whose early movie credits told a French-accented scenario of female daring—*Saint Joan, Bonjour Tristesse, À Bout de Souffle*—paid a heavy price for her high icon adventure. I don't think there's necessarily a lesson here beyond an infinite sadness for the transatlantic romance gone bitterly wrong—and the poignancy of being remembered for a haircut when you wanted so much more. It turned out that even with her beauty and fame, Paris was a tough scene for an American girl who had no one to copy but herself.

In Monday night yoga class, the teacher always tells us not to look at anyone else's pose. Everybody's practice is different, she explains. Naturally, I can't help staring at the young woman with the fabulous body doing a headstand in the middle of the room.

Soon after I returned to New York, Jim married Nathalie, with whom he had a child they called Isaac. The man who wanted to be Jewish got what he wanted and never left Paris. Monique married Alain, became an art historian, and raised two children in Paris, one of whom is my goddaughter and a philosopher. Sixteen years later, I married another unsuitable man with a beard. I'm still married to him.

Not long after I finished the memoir, but long enough after it had settled in my mind as the truth—or at least as much of the truth as I could make mine in a narrative—I received a letter from Nathalie telling me that Jim had died a few months earlier, at age seventy-seven. She had just found my address. The letter from Paris arrived in New York on my birthday.

The last year of his life, she wrote, was long and difficult, but his last weeks were calm and without suffering. She enclosed a recent photograph and, printed on a card bordered in black, Yeats's poem "The Lake Isle of Innisfree," that a friend, she said, had recited at the funeral. I could not read past the first line, "I will arise and go now, and go to Innisfree." I was suddenly choked with grief for the man who, like the poet, never stopped mourning the loss of an Ireland that never would be truly his. I recognized instantly how much Yeats's wish to "live alone in the bee-loud glade" was also Jim's longing for a country he had never possessed, a longing that made the Paris he loved a poor substitute for a native land, though better than exile in America, where he had been born.

In the snapshot taken at an outdoor café, Jim—of course I now desperately want to call him by his name—is wearing a white shirt and tie, as he always did, and a black raincoat. He is heavy, heavier still than when I knew him, and his beard and hair are white. There is just a trace of reddish color in his eyebrows, the remains of a younger palette. His left hand holds the glasses he was always too vain to wear in photographs (I can see the mark made by the nose pads), and in his right, the silver handle of a dark wood walking stick.

Do I know this man? Can you know someone you haven't seen in—in practically a lifetime? The pain in his eyes tells me yes, I do know him, and that, like Colette, I've never gotten over him. I didn't want to say that at the start of my memoir. I substituted Paris for the first husband. It wouldn't have been truthful to say that I was somehow still in love with him. But sitting in my kitchen, as I stared at the photograph, I thought it was true that I never got over the dream we shared: of being the people we never were meant to be in the city we both loved.

So it really happened, I said to myself. The letter from my ex-husband's wife—that must be a modern genre—from my old friend, proves that. She apologizes for sharing her thoughts and memories, but invites me to be in touch when I'm in Paris.

For a long time, I didn't miss Paris and stopped returning. But recently, on a brief stay in London, I made a day trip to Paris on the Eurostar to visit Monique, my old roommate from the Foyer. She was dying of pancreatic cancer, and time was short. Then, last winter, I traveled to Paris and stayed in the apartment where I had once lived too. I slept in the study where Monique wrote her art history books, now a guest room. It was one of those spiral twists that feels like a circle closing, but where you only almost return to the same place. The neighborhood, once shabby and drab, had become chic and fashionable. There was even a café that abutted the apartment building called, in English, the "No Stress Café," a name that would have been incomprehensible in the 1960s, when the resistance to English words was fierce (even if already a losing battle).

Many of the people in this story who mattered to me are dead. I keep losing friends, and that makes me both a mourner and a survivor. But how long before it will be my turn? Sartre said somewhere that the one thing we can't imagine is our own death. And yet it is almost as difficult to take in the death of our friends, our contemporaries, since we are so much like them, since they were so much a part of us.

There's a line I've always loved in *Casablanca* when Humphrey Bogart sadly recognizes that he will not have a future with Ingrid Bergman. "We'll always have Paris," he says, bidding her farewell at the airport. I know what he means.

About the Author

NANCY K. MILLER IS THE author or editor of more than a dozen books, including *What They Saved: Pieces of a Jewish Past*, winner of the Jewish Journal Prize for 2012, and the story of a quest to re-create her family's lost history. A well-known feminist scholar, Miller has published family memoirs, personal essays, and literary criticism. She is a Distinguished Professor of English and Comparative Literature at the Graduate Center, CUNY, where she teaches classes in memoir, graphic novels, and women's studies.

Miller lectures widely, both nationally and internationally, and her work is anthologized in popular volumes on autobiography and collections of feminist essays. She also coedits the Gender and Culture series at Columbia University Press, which she cofounded in 1983 with the late Carolyn Heilbrun.

Visit her at nancykmiller.com.